SECRET EDEN
Africa's Enchanted Wilderness

SECRET

EDEN

Africa's Enchanted Wilderness

Eric Robins

Photographs by Marion Kaplan

Elm Tree Books · London

First published in Great Britain 1980
by Elm Tree Books/Hamish Hamilton Ltd
Garden House 57-59 Long Acre London WC2E 9JZ

Book Design by Norman Reynolds

British Library Cataloguing in Publication Data

Robins, Eric
    Secret Eden.
    1. Selous Game Reserve
    I. Title
    639′.95′09678   SK575.T3
    ISBN 0−241−10423−8

Phototypeset by Filmtype Services Limited, Scarborough
Printed and bound in Hong Kong by
Dai Nippon Printing Co Ltd

Contents

Fish eagle

Author's Note

THERE IS A small and select club – let's call it 'The Company of the Selous' – to which this author and the rest of the world have no qualifications for membership.

The few who do belong nurtured an immense tract of Africa, quite untouched by the twentieth century, and are rightly proud of the special distinction they have earned for themselves. They, I feel, are the real authors of this book, for they were kindly, patient and understanding in guiding me through labyrinths of fact and fantasy, of history and the contemporary scene.

Some of these people appear in the pages ahead, and they certainly appear in the list of acknowledgements below, where there has been no need to specify them as belonging to The Company. Each one knows the others like a devotee of an obscure but exclusive order.

To them, and to all the others listed below from whom I sought help in researching and writing *Secret Eden*, I offer my deepest thanks. To: Solomon Alexander Ole Saibull; Alan Rodgers; Brian Nicholson; Allen Rees; Terry Irwin; Jon Speed; Karl Jahn; Dr Hugh Lamprey, former Director of the Serengeti Research Institute; Judy Houry; Dr Stephen Cobb of Nairobi University, Dr Kim Howell of the University of Dar es Salaam; Mike Clifton of the National Museums of Kenya; Iain Douglas-Hamilton; Sandra Price, Director for Africa of the Washington-based African Wildlife Leadership Foundation; John Capon; Cynthia Moss; Daniel Tarimo; Roger Houghton; veteran hunter Bill Ryan; Dr Bernhard Grzimek; Christian Lysholm; Lars O. Silseth; Frederick Lwezaula, Tanzania's Director of Wildlife; Muhidin Ndolanga, General Manager of the Tanzania Wildlife Corporation; Somi Pallangyo, Sector Manager, Kingupira; Hamisi Faume; Kassim Kagoma; and the staffs of the library of the Royal Commonwealth Society, the Macmillan Library, Nairobi, the Tanzanian Archives and the National Museum of Tanzania in Dar es Salaam.

In a category of his own is the mystery man of Nanyuki, Kenya, who, signing himself 'Mr X', wrote in a neatly typed reply to a newspaper advertisement of mine asking for background information: 'If you wish to know anything about Tanzania's Selous Game Reserve, please write to the above address and I would be only too willing to help as I know the reserve very well.' I replied to the post office box number he gave, stating that I would be most grateful for any material he might have.

I am still wondering as to his identity, career and object in offering assistance for I have had no other word from him!

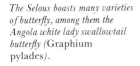

*The Selous boasts many varieties of butterfly, among them the Angola white lady swallowtail butterfly (*Graphium pylades*).*

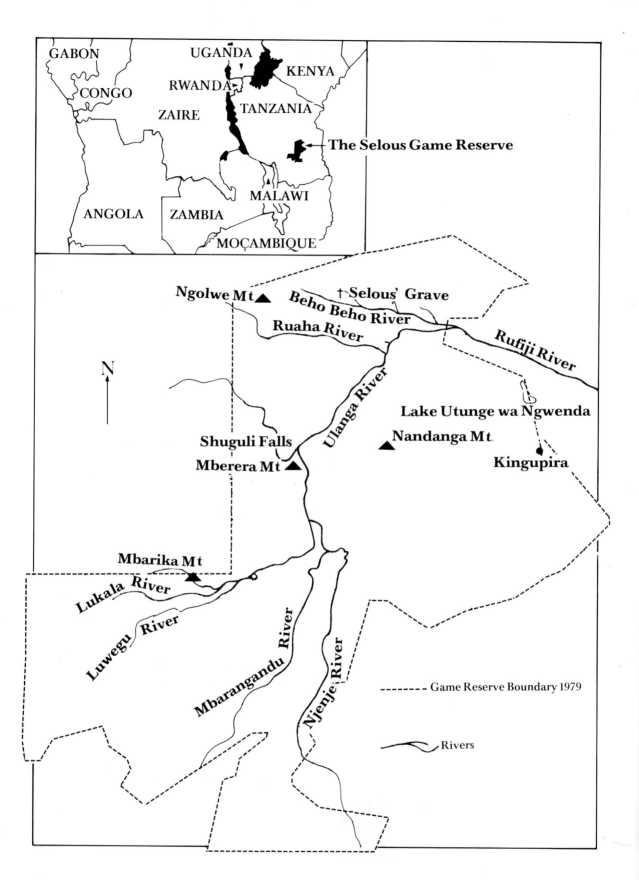

GABON

CONGO

ZAIRE

GABON

UGANDA

RWANDA

KENYA

TANZANIA

The Selous Game Reserve

ANGOLA ZAMBIA

MALAWI

MOÇAMBIQUE

Ngolwe Mt ▲

† Selous' Grave

Beho Beho River

Ruaha River

Rufiji River

N

Ulanga River

Lake Utunge wa Ngwenda

Shuguli Falls

Nandanga Mt ▲

Mberera Mt ▲

Kingupira

Mbarika Mt ▲

Lukala River

Luwegu River

Mbarangandu River

Njenje River

- - - - - Game Reserve Boundary 1979

Rivers

1. 'Karibuni!'

IN A FIERY dawn, the leaves of the hibiscus bush on the platform were covered with pearls of dew and its scarlet flower was a spearhead of folded petals as I stepped down from my train compartment.

The coast's 'Haven of Peace' – Dar es Salaam – was four hours behind me on the arrow-straight, Chinese-built Tazara railway, that covers 1,160 miles of raw Africa to link Zambia's copper mines with Tanzania's Indian Ocean capital.

My Land-Rover, with an amiable Chagga tribesman at the wheel, the forked scars on his face wrinkled in a grin of greeting, stood near the signboard of the little wayside halt with its whitewash and *eau-de-nil* ticket booth, empty waiting-room and a foreman's office where a short-wave radio burped and crackled. The signboard itself – FUGA – had become a rack for a row of sun-bleached buffalo and wildebeest skulls, which littered the surrounding countryside.

In low gear our vehicle lurched and agonized into the bush for a couple of miles, when a length of rusty iron piping between two oil drums, in the shade of an umbrella-shaped acacia tree, barred the track. A well-worn Lee-Enfield rifle slung over his shoulder, a Government game scout, clad in a khaki bush jacket, grey trousers, sandals and a maroon beret with a buffalo-head brass badge, emerged from a reed-thatched mud hut with a dazzling smile and a snappy salute.

Such was the humble gateway to the world's greatest and richest game reserve – the 21,000 square-miles of the Selous (pronounced 'se-loo') in the southern half of East Africa's black socialist republic of Tanzania, claimed by an eminent palaeontologist, Mary Leakey, to have been a cradle of mankind millions of years ago. A vulture flying high above the heart of the reserve (one of Africa's oldest areas devoted to the conservation of all forms of wildlife), would be unable to discern, even with its incredible vision, the Selous' borders which run 200 miles to the north and south.

Home of more than a million creatures, including the largest African elephant population on earth, the Selous is so vast – bigger than Denmark, twice the size of Maryland state – and so devoid of human habitation, that nature remains completely in balance. As

proof of this the animals, with very few exceptions, are in prime condition. Shaped like a surrealist pelican and named after a Victorian hunter-explorer who turned conservationist, it has the continent's biggest crocodile, hippo, wild dog and buffalo concentrations. In one area of 400 square miles – taken at random – Tanzanian game officials recently counted 30,000 animals, among them 2,349 zebra, 2,500 buffalo, 200 hippo, 650 elephant, 6,649 impala, 61 lions, and 6,364 wildebeest and hartebeest.

With all settlement now banned, there are no endangered animals in the Selous Game Reserve. In fact, all the species are increasing in numbers in a panoramic Eden that ranges from vast undulating plains dotted with steely-blue lakes to cloud-ringed mountains; from palmy forests and the rocky massifs of Nandanga, Mbarika, Mberera and Ngolwe – names like an African chant – to a network of great rivers and sheer gorges boiling with white water.

Despite the richness of its fauna and flora, the Selous kingdom remained virtually unknown over the years except to a few hundred big game hunters, ecologists, botanists, geologists and a handful of other hardy trail-blazers.

Moneyed sportsmen, who knew the Selous as a place for record animal trophies, were inclined to keep the secret to themselves, but now impoverished Tanzania, with a population of 18 million peasant farmers, is promoting tourism to earn foreign exchange that will help build sorely-needed schools, hospitals, community centres and maternity clinics.

Great regions of the Selous' 21,000 square miles are eerie and mysterious and, unlike most game reserves, all of it is unpopulated.

The Selous, the world's largest game reserve: its perpetual viability is guaranteed by its multiple rivers.

10

Lake Tagalala, one of a series of lakes in the northern Selous fed by the Rufiji river, at the heart of some of the loveliest tourist country.

No one lives in the Selous but a few game scouts are posted there and hunters and their licensed clients pass through. Road signs are few, small and have been in place for many years.

'*Karibuni* – Come in!' the game scout shouted a welcome in Swahili as he pulled aside the iron bar to let the Land-Rover pass.

Although bustling Dar es Salaam with its wide streets, modern hotels and office blocks lay only seventy-odd miles to the north-east, when I entered the Selous I felt like an explorer – an intruder even. In this game reserve the lives of the beasts and exotic birds had not changed for countless centuries.

Under an implacable sky, a brooding silence hung over a blanket of golden grass which stretched as far as the eye could see. As we rattled along a sandy track through an avenue of *mopani* trees, a line of heliotrope hills, drenched in sunlight, came into view. Between them flowed the broad, coffee-brown Rufiji river, one of the reserve's half-a-dozen waterways.

Travelling deeper into the bush, we skirted riverine marshes and seemingly boundless lakes in which the dead, ashen poles of flooded palms stood like gaunt sentinels. Where the earth's crust was thin, sulphurous hot springs bubbled and steamed between scabrous green, black and grey rocks.

Five hours after leaving Fuga, we parked in the cool shade of a grove of mango trees for a lunch of goat-milk cheese sandwiches, bananas and a pineapple.

The trees with their heavy, dark-green foliage had a sad history, said the Chagga driver. They had grown up from the stones of the sweet, blush-skinned fruit dropped by groups of black men, women and children who were victims of the nineteenth-century slave trade. The hapless captives, squatting in wooden halters, ate the fruit to ward off starvation on their way from the interior to the Indian Ocean, where the foetid holds of Arab merchants' dhows with their sharkfin sails awaited them. The mango trees of the Selous are constant reminders of the ghastly era when merchants traded in human flesh.

In the north near Beho Beho are several hidden springs. This lush place, with palms and boulders rounded by water, is one. Others lead to pools deep enough to bathe in.

2. Deutschland Uber Ostafrika

TOWARDS THE END of the nineteenth century, a German scholar named Dr Carl Peters cast covetous eyes over what is today mainland Tanzania, for the thin-lipped Doctor of Philosophy and author of several high-minded papers on metaphysics was also a rabid colonialist. For the greater glory of the Reich (and Dr Peters), he envisaged under the German eagle a land that is a key in itself to a riddle of man's origins: 362,000 square miles, just below the Equator, made up of a silvery coastal strip 600 miles long, lined with palms; an internal plateau 3,000 feet high; waterless semi-deserts; an inland sea (Lake Victoria now) encircled by papyrus beds; open parkland teeming with elephant, lion, rhino and giraffe; tangled forests; verdant highlands, and craggy mountain ranges.

The academic imperialist, his choleric greed matched only by that of the other European empire builders of the same era, wasted no time in achieving a classic commercial conquest. Having formed a private organization known as the Society for German Colonisation, Dr Peters in 1884 led armed expeditions into the heartland. In the name of the Fatherland, he traded hollow 'treaties of protection' with drunken, illiterate or greedy native chiefs in return for 'thumb-signed' documents giving him and his society overlordship of a territory the size of France and Germany put together.

Kaiser Wilhelm I granted a charter to Peters' rag-bag of German businessmen out for a quick kill, and the 'Society' became the German East Africa Company.

Germany had been the last of the European nations to enter the Scramble for Africa. She owed her colonial possessions in east and south-west Africa more to such commercial enterprises as those of Peters than to explorers, missionaries, or the military – the accepted order of conquest.

The early German settlers in East Africa had a creed which was spelt out in stark Gothic type:

The task of the coloniser is wide and diversified. The natives are ignorant. They must be instructed. They are indolent. They must be taught to work. They are unclean. They must be taught

15

cleanliness. They are ill with all manner of distempers. They must be healed. They are savage, cruel and superstitious. They must become peaceful and enlightened.

The G.E.A.C. (German East Africa Company) proclaimed anti-slavery measures, then introduced even more barbaric cruelties than those practised by the Arabs. Dr Peters and his 5,000-odd followers ushered in a regime of death and bloodshed throughout the sunny land. Thousands of blacks were hanged from acacia trees at a whim. Others were flogged to death with rhino-hide whips. Corpses were left spread-eagled on wagon wheels as grim warnings to the rebellious. Forced labour, under appalling conditions, in which countless thousands died, helped to 'pacify' seven million Africans.

This was Peters' reasoning, but the excesses of his rule drove at least one section of the oppressed population to rise in revolt: a ragged company of blacks and Arabs ran amok, massacred whites on the dusty streets and set the Company's coffee and sisal plantations ablaze. But the revolt was swiftly and mercilessly put down by bullet and sword. Its leader, Bushiri bin Salim, was hanged in public and his body left to the vultures.

In 1891 the Kaiser's government formally took over the running of German East Africa from the G.E.A.C. It then became a main zone of Teutonic colonization in Africa.

During this time both Britain and Germany were heavily engaged in the scramble for African possessions and the Kaiser complained to his aunt, Queen Victoria, that *two* mountains were included within the borders of Her Majesty's colony of Kenya: Mount Kenya and Mount Kilimanjaro. As a result, Queen Victoria gave the Kaiser a truly magnanimous gift as a status symbol – the snow-domed Kilimanjaro, at 19,430 feet Africa's highest peak and later made famous by the American author, Ernest Hemingway, in his novel *The Snows of Kilimanjaro*.

With a nucleus of 2,000 government administrators and military men, the new German colony began to progress, although imports far exceeded exports and it remained for many years in the red in the Treasury ledgers in Berlin.

Deplorably, the story of calculated harshness towards the 'protected' Africans continued. The evil Carl Peters, with his mass executions and mortal whippings, was still very much in evidence and although the man was finally sacked from the German colonial service as a result of the outcries back home, his 'civilizing' abuses continued under brutish white officials.

African men and women were kidnapped to provide dirt cheap (or unpaid) labour on farms set up across land seized from the various tribes. Labourers, who worked from sunrise to dusk seven days a week for handfuls of maize, were chained and flogged almost to death on any suspicion of malingering or resistance to the sadistic system. Inevitably, there was a series of native uprisings; all were ruthlessly put down.

A scarab beetle with fierce pincers and spear-like antennae.

16

The worst of these conflicts took place when the whole of the southern half of the colony exploded. In what was known as the Maji-Maji Rebellion, howling, spear-waving tribesmen advanced against lines of German troops in what became suicide squads. *Maji* is Swahili for 'water' and witchdoctors who sold gourds of 'sacred' water to the credulous for a chicken or a sack of sweet potatoes, said the potions would turn the German bullets to water if drunk or poured over a man's body. (Some of the water came from those volcanic springs now within the Selous.) But, although wave after wave of charging Africans was cut down, thousands of fanatical rebels stormed and sacked German garrisons in Beau Geste-type forts.

There were brutalities on both sides. The Maji-Maji fighters slaughtered entire families of whites and their Arab servants; the Germans responded with a ferocity that more than matched the enemy. Tribal villages – with the inhabitants still in their reed-thatched mud huts – were put to the torch, along with subsistence maize and cassava plantations. Tens of thousands of Africans died in the subsequent famine and epidemics of disease.

Three years after the captured Maji-Maji leaders had mounted the scaffold in 1907, the Kaiser gave his wife a wedding anniversary present – undoubtedly one of the biggest of its kind in the annals of romance. This was an area of land in the southern half of German East Africa. Roughly bounded by four rivers, it contained such a variety of wild animals that it was both a teeming natural zoo and a hunter's dream. This was the nucleus of the present Selous Game Reserve. After World War I, both the British and later an independent African government added more and more land to the Kaiser's gift which is still known to the older tribespeople in the area as 'Shamba Ya Bibi' (the 'Woman's Field').

For a few years, until the outbreak of the war, German East Africa entered a period of tranquillity as the administrators adopted a relatively liberal policy of providing basic, higher and technical education. They introduced, under an experimental 'scientific colonialism' programme, an enlightened economic and social form of imperialism. With self-interest and typical efficiency, the Germans trained the tribesmen to fight for, and not against, them. They formed platoons of *schwartztruppe* who were to become the goose-stepping elite of black fighting men. Constant floggings kept them, literally, on their toes.

Following a wave of revulsion in Europe against the mass extermination of the Herero tribespeople in South-West Africa by General von Trotha (on whose staff in 1904 was a brilliant junior officer named Paul von Lettow-Vorbeck) and the scorched earth method of stamping out the ashes of the Maji-Maji uprising, measures were taken to improve the situation. Harsh and incompetent civil servants were summarily dismissed from the German colonial administration, the use of forced labour was outlawed, and all work contracts had to be approved by the government. Flogging, medically supervised, was

17

allowed only for major crimes. Land-grabbing by whites was banned by law, and Africans were encouraged to grow cash crops. There was also substantial economic and agricultural progress, and the sisal, cotton, tobacco, rubber, sugar and coffee plantations around stout, white-walled German farmsteads began to provide bountiful harvests.

By early 1914 German East Africa was being opened up to full commercial exploitation by the building, under particularly gruelling conditions, of two great railroads linking the coast and the interior.

In flag-bedecked Dar es Salaam, among cubist forts and 'Hansel and Gretel' churches, sat the new Commander-in-Chief of East Africa. He was that 44-year-old bush war veteran from South-West Africa, Colonel – soon to be General – von Lettow-Vorbeck.

With his close-cropped hair, hooked nose, piercing gaze and ramrod stiffness, von Lettow, a general's son, looked every inch the Prussian autocrat he was. True to type, he was haughty and arrogant, but imbued with a redeeming if somewhat misplaced sense of chivalry. In the forthcoming war with Britain he was to prove himself a man of superhuman endurance with a guerrilla's skill, eclipsing that in later years of Mao-tse Tung or Che Guevéra, and a knight's gallantry. Indeed, von Lettow emerged as one of the most famous names in German military history and, like Rommel, the 'Desert Fox' of World War II, became a popular hero of both sides.

The Königsberg – *once the pride of Germany's Indian Ocean battle fleet, was finally sunk in the Rufiji Delta in World War I.* Kenya Railways.

Holding the stage for four years throughout the whole of the First World War, he waged one of the most successful bush-fighter's campaigns ever mounted. With inadequate weapons and no hope of reinforcements for his brave little force, he made the British maintain in the East African theatre of war an army equivalent in size to that which was needed to defeat the Boers years earlier in South Africa.

It was a tough and crazy war that von Lettow fought – a war where the enemy painted mules with black and white stripes to disguise them as zebras, where naval guns from a wrecked warship were pressed into field service, and black soldiers on scouting forays were dressed up as witchdoctors in hideous wooden masks, python skins and ostrich feathers.

The battlefields ranged from thick forest to thorn-scrub and stony hills. Troops had to endure the Turkish-bath heat of the coastal belt, the torrid sun of the central plateau and the icy mists of the highlands.

For the German commander, transport, water and food supply problems were as immense and variable as the territory over which he fought.

Early in the Great War, however, little attention was directed towards this military wizard and his will-o-the-wisp *askaris* (African soldiers) for the world's gaze was focused on a ship, a 'phantom raider'. She was the *Königsberg*, a fast light cruiser of the German Navy with ten 4.1-inch guns, torpedo tubes and a crew of 350. Her prominence in the international press was due to the fact that she was preying at will on Allied shipping in the Indian Ocean.

Hunted by a gaggle of British cruisers eager to blow her out of the water, this deadly greyhound continued to deal heavy blows to the enemy's sea power under the daring and skilful command of Captain Looff.

Badly needing a refit after a whole year at sea creating havoc among merchant and naval vessels alike (Looff even sank a British warship in harbour at Zanzibar for good measure), the 3,400-ton *Königsberg* dodged her would-be captors and inched her way into the noisome delta of the surging, 400-mile-long Rufiji river which runs through the heart of what is now the Selous. (The delta itself, the largest of its kind in East Africa, is close to the north-east boundary of the reserve.)

Captain Looff's navigation in this instance alone was a maritime feat. Although the delta was an ideal hiding place for the dhows of Arab slavers, it is by no means an appropriate retreat for a man-o'-war and her crew.

Although it was to serve the *Königsberg's* purpose well, the Rufiji delta is a nightmare translated into reality – a rain-lashed maze of

shoals, sandbars, rip tides, eddies and brackish ever-changing channels. It is a poisonous morass of palm-fringed creeks, either boiling
with crocodiles or buried under rotting jungles. There are awesome
thunderstorms and heavy squalls almost every day, and when the sun
forces its way through ink-black clouds the delta floats in foetid mists.

Monkeys scream among the matted and bearded trees and long
thorns tear at the thighs of intruders. Blood-sucking leeches, six
inches long, abound in the deep mud that forms two-thirds of the
delta and provides a breeding ground for the mosquitoes which carry
malaria. Elephants crash through the undergrowth, while the young,
the sick and the old sink and are drowned in the ooze. Clouds of
mosquitoes attack their human victims with almost tigerish ferocity,

*Like a ball of fire the
Haemanthus lily (*Scadoxus
multiflorus*) bursts from the
damp soil at the beginning of the
rains.*

leaving a man's arms and legs black with blood, and enraged hippo charge and overturn the frail craft of native fishermen in a bid to crush them in their steel-vice jaws.

'If in this world there is a worse place than the Rufiji delta, I hope I may never find it,' wrote Commander Alan Villiers who roamed the globe under sail. 'The whole delta is gloomy, morose and depressing almost beyond endurance.'

The miasma of the place (in so vivid a contrast to the adjoining Selous) affected Captain Looff and his men in much the same way. But, driven by the necessity created by a flotilla of British naval vessels lurking offshore, they quickly hacked down branches and bushes with axes and *pangas* (machetes) and covered the cruiser's decks with them.

In the eyes of the British, the badly wanted 'phantom' had vanished once more. What followed was to be the longest naval engagement in history, spread over more than eight months, before they were able to wipe out the raider.

The first clue as to the *Königsberg's* hideaway came when a British patrol boat captured a German tug whose papers showed she had taken coal to the cruiser six miles up the delta.

Air reconnaissance in Africa was born. The British navy pressed into service a South African civilian who owned a gimcrack, 90 h.p. seaplane. Having given him a lieutenant's commission for the occasion, they ordered him to fly over the tortuous unmapped delta.

After a series of hair's breadth escapes from death as he zoomed above the tree tops, the dashing pilot of the flying stringbag spotted the German cruiser's topmast protruding from a mass of greenery. Making a spectacular crash-landing in the sea, he clambered out of the sinking wreckage and excitedly reported his discovery to the British admiral.

That, nevertheless, was less, far less, than half the battle.

3. End of a Legend

LURKING IN THE green hell of the Rufiji delta a decade or so before the 1914 war was a slightly-built, softly-spoken man in his early forties, who looked timorous enough to be frightened by a male baboon.

The appearance was deceptive. Leathery Pieter Pretorius richly deserved his reputation as one of Africa's greatest elephant hunters. A descendant of the Boer general who gave his name to South Africa's administrative capital of Pretoria, P.P., lithe, with a skin yellowish-brown from continual bouts of malaria, shot hundreds of elephants during his career – the majority for their ivory – on the banks of the Rufiji river or among the serpentine creeks of the delta, and once survived a charge of *five* enraged elephants.

Pretorius was an unassuming and gentle man whose marksmanship was so superb that his targets rarely suffered but, in 1906, the Germans aroused his ire by confiscating his small hunting lodge on the edge of the delta because he refused to sell the property to a Prussian army officer. Pieter Pretorius swore revenge, and the Germans were to regret their high-handed confiscation – he called it 'theft' – of his home.

As a first stage, he mounted a wholesale killing of elephants in the German territory. Then came World War I and Pretorius's unique opportunity for full retribution.

Way down in South Africa, the British authorities had been inclined to regard Pretorius, with his family background of opposition in the Boer War, as a German spy, although nothing could have been further from the truth. But when Rear-Admiral Herbert King-Hall, who was in charge of the sea blockade of the *Königsberg*, heard of the jungle man's vow to get even with the Germans, the old sailor welcomed the news as a means at last to destroy the bottled-up cruiser.

P.P. was an enthusiastic recruit to the British cause, and he set about the tasks given him by the admiral with characteristic daring and vigour. He became the first big game hunter ever to stalk a warship – an entirely new tactic, never before used by a navy anywhere!

An elephant among the strange borassus palms of the Selous.

P.P. knew more about the Rufiji delta, its depths and convoluted

Elephant and calf browsing along the banks of the Mbarangandu river. To this day many species of grasses are undiscovered and unnamed.

sandy bends, than any man alive, and the hunter, who could virtually communicate with wild beasts, was also the *rafiki* (friend) of thousands of tribespeople in the region. He looked and lived like a light-skinned African and had an uncanny sixth sense of danger.

His first mission was to fix the location of the *Königsberg* in the primeval slime: she had crept further down the delta from her original position spotted by that intrepid young man in his float-fitted flying machine. Pretorius chose as his companions for the venture, 'six of the biggest rogues on the east coast'. But, as he pointed out, what they lacked in morals they made up for in courage and tenacity of purpose.

The first thing the villainous-looking party discovered was a series of deserted villages that the Germans had cleared to ensure that the inhabitants did not disclose the ship's whereabouts. Ironically, the empty huts provided the Afrikaner scout with confirmation that the *Königsberg* was still hiding in the sodden maze.

Under cover of darkness, and at the height of a thunderstorm, P.P. and his men made their way inland by dug-out canoe and on their bare feet. Two black porters carrying supplies of fruit on their heads to the cruiser were seized. With knives at their throats, the captives were forced to guide Pretorius to a hillock seventeen miles inland. Perched in a mango tree at dawn, Pretorius could see the grey 'sea monster' less than 300 yards away. The *Königsberg's* decks were smothered in lopped branches, bushes and hacked-down trees, her sides painted green to match the palm forest around.

A raised trunk sniffs the air indicating nervousness and a sense of alarm. There's no threat here, just awareness of an unfamiliar presence.

Pretorius was welcomed back by the British as a hero, and was eventually awarded the army rank of major and a Distinguished Service Order medal with bar. But his hazardous tasks were not over. The next assignment given him by the admiral was to discover what guns the *Königsberg* still mounted, and whether her torpedoes were still aboard.

Dodging all the German sentries with consummate bushcraft, he crept back to his old vantage point and, during a deluge, trained his binoculars on the cruiser. There, right under his nose, were her eight remaining 4-inch guns and rain-sodden sailors at their posts on deck.

P.P. went back to the coast to take on his bravest role yet.

Donning the long, dirty-white robes of an Arab poultry trader ('I needed no skin colouring – twenty-five years in the African sun had provided that'), he press-ganged an African chief, who was in fact an old friend, into posing as his servant and the pair set out with the gift of a basket of chickens for the cruiser's men.

Pretorius was in luck once more. One of the chief's sons had been forced to work as a stoker aboard the trapped *Königsberg*. On this account alone, the old headman had no love for the Germans.

The chief and Pretorius, ostensibly en route inland to barter fowls for eggs, approached the cruiser, nodding and bowing to the unsuspecting sentries.

Given permission to leave the ship for a brief reunion with his father, the chief's son was brought into the charade. Playing his part

27

bravely, the young man hugged his father who, under the eyes of the Germans, whispered in the vernacular: 'Where are the long bullets that swim in the water?'

Pretorius squatted on the ground and seemed to take no interest in the emotional family scene.

The son replied, again in the native language, that some of the warship's torpedoes had been removed from the ship and set up close to the Rufiji mouth to be fired point blank at any approaching British naval vessels.

After a tearful leave-taking, the chief and Pretorius went off with this vital information and made their way back to the admiral.

He was delighted, but still hungry for information about his prey. Determined that when he finally made his move the *Königsberg* would be doomed, he sent Pretorius back into the trees to risk crocodiles, mines and pythons – not to mention summary execution by a German naval firing squad as a spy.

Day after day, within sight and sound of the enemy, Pretorius worked with a 12-foot pole in a dug-out canoe taking soundings in order to find navigable channels up which the British navy could sail to strike against the raider. Sun-bronzed and wearing only a flimsy loin-cloth, the dauntless agent looked like any other African fisherman searching for catfish and bream. P.P. exchanged waves and smiles with members of the crew lining the cruiser's rails as he sealed the *Königsberg's* death warrant with his explorations; they did not seem to find it strange that he rarely caught any fish.

With great courage he paced out the distance from the cruiser to a large sandbank, then found a seven-mile-long channel down which shallow-draft vessels from the coast could navigate in six to seven feet of water. From the sandbank, the *Königsberg* would be within range of 6-inch guns.

Using a crude chart prepared by the elephant hunter, the captains of two British naval monitors drawing but a few feet of water navigated their craft close to the doomed cruiser, now little better than a steel coffin filled with sick and dying men.

In a final act of bravery, just before the real drama began, Pretorius allowed himself to be used as a decoy in a dhow to draw the German's fire. Miraculously, he escaped unhurt under a hail of machine-gun bullets and rifle fire from the banks as the monitors, *Severn* and *Mersey*, guided by an observer plane, opened fire. This barrage was immediately answered by the *Königsberg's* own heavy armament.

Four hours later, the duel was over. The *Königsberg's* guns and the land batteries were silenced, her back was broken and her gallant Captain Looff gravely wounded. His last act of defiance was to explode one of his ship's own torpedoes in the engine-room, and she slowly listed over – a blazing twisted hulk – in the swirling muddy waters (where her rust-red outline can still be seen).

The German threat in the Indian Ocean was over, and Pieter

Pretorius had settled his score with the Kaiser. The tide of fortune was beginning to turn too against the cunning and courtly von Lettow and his vastly outnumbered force. Making a series of strategic withdrawals to the south, he was obliged to salvage a couple of the *Königsberg's* guns and turn them into field pieces, for the German land forces now had to reckon with a new adversary, just as formidable as Pretorius, and once a distinguished member of the same ivory-hunting profession.

Frederick Courteney Selous, long-famed throughout the African *bundu* (bush), now appeared in the theatre of war. A vigorous man in his early sixties, Selous was actually of Norman-French descent although, incongruously, he appeared to be an eccentric cross between the perfect English gentleman and the popular conception of Buffalo Bill. His father's family – from Jersey in the Channel Islands – were Huguenots driven from France by the Revocation of the Edict of Nantes. His mother, keenly interested in animal and plant life whose 'whole soul shrank away from any form of killing', was the daughter of an English farmer. When Frederick was born on 31 December 1851 (in a mansion in Regent's Park near the site of the present London zoo), his father was a prominent stockbroker who collected butterflies as an outdoor hobby.

Frederick Courteney Selous in 1917, three days before his death in action. Kenya Railways.

Hot-tempered and adventurous as a boy, Frederick Selous was constantly in trouble at his English boarding school. He was once found sleeping on the bare dormitory floor because 'one day I am going to be a hunter in Africa'.

His Gallic-sounding name marked him among his snobbish school-fellows as 'not a pure-blooded Englishman'. (This may have given rise in later years in South Africa – where there were interbred Huguenot and black families – to the myth that he was a Coloured, or man of mixed blood. Certainly the combination of malarial attacks – quietened with massive doses of quinine – with which he was afflicted during his career in Africa, and the constant tanning of the sun, made his skin very definitely off-white.) However, tormented at school as 'a frog-eating Frenchy', he developed a personality and character more English than the English.

He was an ardent naturalist like his mother and father (and a crack shot to boot) even before entering Rugby – the famous English public school where the game originated – in January 1866.   An avid reader (under the bedclothes in his dormitory) of the exploits in Africa of the Scottish missionary-explorer, young Selous told his housemaster firmly: 'I mean to be like Dr Livingstone.'

F.C. Selous left Rugby at the age of seventeen, and his parents sent him to Europe to learn French and German, and how to play the violin. They wanted him to become a doctor, but his real interests on the Continent were hunting – or poaching chamois – shooting and fishing. During the hours he should have spent studying medicine, he was searching for birds' nests in the woods or chasing butterflies. Clearly, Frederick Selous was not destined for the operating theatre or the consulting room.

*Selous' father was a collector of British butterflies. Here, in Africa, is a citrus swallowtail butterfly (*Papilio demodocus*).*

He had become an accomplished musician and was fluent in several languages, but his imagination had been fired by the adventures of the great lion and elephant hunters of his day. He burned his medical books – if not his boats – and left home, arriving by ship at Algoa Bay in South Africa in September 1871, with only £400 in his pocket, determined to follow in the footsteps of his heroes.

To that end, the young man had already acquired the bushy beard, bush hat, khaki shorts and bush jacket that were the trappings of the breed. His eyes were already 'as clear and blue as a summer sky'.

Using powerful large-bore guns 'with a kick like two mules', Selous began his incredible life as a hunter and ivory trader by killing seventy-seven elephant within two years. There were so many of them around him in southern Africa that he believed he would never reduce their numbers, no matter how many he killed.

When his horse became exhausted, Selous would leap from the saddle. Wearing only a shirt and sandals, he pursued his quarry on foot and closing in on the animal at full tilt, he would load his gun from a powder bag, slither to a stop and fire at point-blank range. Later, he was to use a smooth, 4-bore duck gun to bring down his victims.

Buffalo along the banks of the Rufiji river in a wild flower garden.

During his hunting years in Africa, the redoubtable Selous and his wiry terrier, Punch, roamed far and wide and had a thousand narrow escapes from savage buffalo, charging rhino, marauding lions, grief-maddened elephant and murderous tribesmen with their war-spears and clubs.

This 'Prince Among Men', as he was dubbed by the Press back home, became a close friend through an exchange of letters of the then American president, Theodore (Teddy) Roosevelt, another naturalist-hunter, and of famous black chiefs like King Khama, Lewanika, and the warrior Lobengula ('Calf of the Black Cow').

F. C. Selous was an imperialist associate of Cecil John Rhodes who used him shamelessly for his own grandiose ends. Selous, not Rhodes, was perhaps the true founder of Rhodesia, now known as Zimbabwe. Although frequently critically ill with malaria he contracted in the Zambesi valley, Selous opened up thousands of miles of south-central Africa to the white man. His discoveries, including a vast underground lake of cobalt-blue waters and a mountain that he named after Darwin, were honoured by the Royal Geographical Society in London who awarded him their coveted gold medal.

31

Back in England, after playing a storybook hero's role against *impis* (battalions) of fierce black warriors in the Matabele War (the white and black commandos, who gave no quarter in their battles against African guerrillas in Rhodesia a century later, were inappropriately named after him), Selous declared: 'I am not a fighting man. I neither look forward with any enthusiasm to the prospect of being shot, nor feel any strong desire to shoot anyone else.'

He courted and married an English clergyman's daughter in February 1874. After a honeymoon in Venice, he took his bride with him back to Rhodesia – a hard, dangerous land for pioneers and their wives.

Selous, a prolific writer who was to become the author of several popular books based on his life on safari, corresponded regularly with President Teddy Roosevelt, who made him a 'never-more-welcome' guest at the White House in Washington. Roosevelt, a puny, seven-stone weakling as a child, with poor eyesight, who became a towering international figure, publicly described his friend as 'the greatest of the world's big game hunters'. Selous modestly denied this.

As a result of their comradeship and the hunter's fascinating stories about the bush, in 1909 the then ex-President asked Selous to arrange a hunting trip in East Africa for himself and his son, Kermit.

Selous bought ridgebacks and other hunting dogs, and stout-hearted horses. He kitted out Roosevelt and the boy with sun helmets,

Teddy Roosevelt, former US President and intrepid big game hunter (far left), shares the cowcatcher of an East African train in 1909 with colonial administrators and Selous (second from right). Kenya Railways.

bandoliers, safari suits and snake-boots and organized a caravan of 500 African porters, each with a sixty-pound headload.

The American's ambition was to shoot a lion – any lion, male or female; black-maned or otherwise. With Selous' coaching, he and Kermit shot seven in one hunting block alone and, ever anxious to assert his manhood, Teddy Roosevelt speared lions on foot. This was a gladiatorial gesture of courage as Selous had warned his friend that, of all animals, he considered the lion to be by far the most dangerous.

Returning home via Khartoum, Roosevelt wrote: 'There are no words that can tell the hidden spirit of the wilderness, that can reveal its mystery, its melancholy and its charm. There is delight in the hardy life of the open, in long rides – rifle in hand – in the thrill of the fight with dangerous game.

'Apart from this, yet mingled with it, is the strong attraction of the silent places, of the large tropic moons and the splendour of the stars where the wanderer sees the awful glory of sunrise and in the wide spaces of the earth, unworn of Man, and changed only by the slow change of the eyes through time everlasting.'

Selous by then had shot between 300 and 400 elephant, lion, buffalo and rhino since the start of his hunting career. Accused in some quarters in Britain of being 'a blood-thirsty murderer' after he had confessed in one of his books that he had slaughtered 548 wild animals in a three-year period, Selous retorted that, apart from the 'kaffirs' in his employ as gunbearers, cooks and porters, he had to provide meat for hordes of hungry 'savages' who accompanied him on his expeditions, uninvited, and relied on him for their daily food.

A well-weathered black-maned lion. Jon Speed.

Frederick Courteney Selous had been a harsh critic of his country's actions in South Africa which led to the Boer War, but he boarded a steamer and returned to England to volunteer for service in the army as World War I drew near. However, both the War Office and Lord Kitchener rejected him as (he said) 'a useless old buffer' so he became a special constable in Pirbright, but continued knocking on the doors of Whitehall with that resolute determination that characterized his life. Finally, Selous was accepted for service and he was shipped off to East Africa as a lieutenant in the Legion of Frontiersmen, the 25th Royal Fusiliers.

Selous landed at Kenya's Indian Ocean port of Mombasa with a motley company of trigger-happy individuals. They numbered among their ranks a lion-tamer, a heavyweight American millionaire, deserters from the French Foreign Legion, a circus clown, an opera tenor, zoo and lighthouse keepers, four music-hall acrobats, a London policeman, and a former general in the Honduran army (who was to become a sergeant).

There were Arabs, Afrikaners, West Indians, Sikhs, Nigerians and Irishmen among the men going to help crush the wily General von Lettow-Vorbeck who had constantly trounced and outwitted Britain and her allies in the sweltering East African cockpit.

Far from the pock-marked quagmires of the battlefields of France, it was a war of venture and initiative fought over vast, sun-baked distances of unknown and unmapped terrain. There were strange horrors such as snakes that lay coiled like cow-pats and struck to kill in seconds, man-eating lions and armies of all-consuming soldier ants. The dangers provided by nature were often worse than those posed by the enemy. It was a war in a brutal climate of searing heat carrying fatal diseases that have only recently been brought under control. Mysterious jungle sicknesses killed off men and left the survivors hollow-eyed living skeletons. At other times they were up to their chests in foetid mangrove swamps, attacked by crocodiles or pythons, and prey to vampire leeches while, as Selous light-heartedly described things, 'bullets swept over us in bouquets'.

'We have wild animals as well as wild devils to fight,' his colonel told the generals.

34

Sporting a goatee beard like his own leader, General Smuts, the sleeves of his unbuttoned shirt – now with a captain's three 'pips' – rolled up, his rifle slung over his shoulder and a twinkle in his eye even on the darkest days, the indomitable Selous marched hour after hour with his men. He boasted he was never a moment off duty, this 'useless old buffer'.

'But,' he wrote to a friend from the ragged African frontline, 'once I'm through with this job, no more military duty for me. I hate all the drill and routine work, and I shall be far too old to take part in any war after this one. This bush-work is very trying as the German *askaris* (African soldiers) are much better at it than heavily-equipped white men, many of whom have always lived in towns. They [the *askaris*] are recruited from fighting tribes, and are not only very brave but very well armed.'

Having escaped the worst of the afflictions that struck down his men – heat-stroke, dysentery, blackwater fever, typhus and others – Selous quite miserably and unromantically developed piles.

When he returned to the East African battle scene in June 1916, after a successful operation in London, Smuts had captured a large stretch of land, from Dar es Salaam to Mount Kilimanjaro, from the Germans.

In January 1917, a company led by Captain Selous, now a holder of the Distinguished Service Order, was commanded to take part in a major offensive to drive von Lettow far south. So what is now the Selous game reserve became an arena of human conflict.

Escaping encirclement, the Germans took up positions with machine-gun nests and riflemen entrenched on a wooded ridge of the Sugar Mountain in the Beho Beho area. There are conflicting reports – some gilded by time, perhaps – of what followed.

The popular version of the action is that Selous, after signalling his sick and weary fusiliers to stand ready for action, loped forward in his unmilitary shirt and shorts, slouch hat and silk scarf knotted round his neck to spy out the positions of the German's strong rearguard. As he raised his field-glasses, the 65-year-old scout was struck in the mouth by a sniper's bullet and died instantly.

Another less inspiring tale of his death was told to white hunter Stanley Lawrence-Brown of Kenya by a snowy-haired old African who claimed to have been a batman with Selous' troop. According to him, Selous was advancing with his soldiers in the afternoon when, like a true Englishman, he ordered a halt to 'brew up' tea. There was no firing then but, later, when he was sitting on an ammunition box drinking from an enamel mug, he was struck in the chest by a sniper's bullet. Standing up to direct his corporal to the marksman, the story goes, he was struck in the head by a second bullet and died where he fell.

Another story that may also be apocryphal is that Selous' native gunbearer ran amok after his master had been killed, and dashed into the German lines where he hacked down half-a-dozen officers and men before being shot in the heart.

Whatever the true facts, Captain Selous' body was sewn up in a grey army blanket and buried under a cairn of stones at the exact spot where he died.

He was mourned by both sides. The shock of his death spread throughout the entire British force, and von Lettow, who was to say after the war that 'Selous was well known among us on account of his charming manner and exciting stories', found time to telegraph a message of condolence and regret to the British as he retreated across the Rufiji river.

Later a simple wooden cross was set on the cairn which marked the spot where Selous 'slept under the wide and starry sky in the Africa he loved so well'.

In his epitaph, President Roosevelt wrote:

Selous' grave, near Beho Beho in the northern part of the reserve, today is marked by a simple slab of cement. An unknown hand has placed some wild daisies on the stone.

It is well for any country to produce men of such a type, and if there are enough of them the nation need fear no decadence.

Frederick Courteney Selous led a singularly adventurous and fascinating life with just the right alternations between the wilderness and civilization.

He helped spread the borders of his people's land. He added much to the sum of human knowledge and interest.

He closed his life exactly as such a life ought to be closed – by dying in battle for his country while rendering her valiant and effective service.

By then von Lettow, wracked by malaria, was little more than a yellow-skinned wraith. He lived like his *askaris* (he called them his 'children' while they in turn revered him) on hippo and elephant meat.

His entire military strength had been reduced to 300 whites and 11,000 Africans; they faced 300,000 troops led by 137 allied commanders. But von Lettow was never defeated by these vastly superior forces. He surrendered only when Germany collapsed in Europe and the armistice was signed. He was lauded by Smuts and other former foes as a noble soldier.

In his last years von Lettow's code of honour remained untarnished. Scorning an ambassadorial post in the Nazi regime offered personally by Adolf Hitler, the aged general lost his pension and was forced to take work as a gardener.

4. 'This Precious Inheritance'

CONQUERED GERMAN EAST Africa was a grim place at the time of the Kaiser's surrender in 1918. Ruined or abandoned plantations were everywhere. The victors seized stocks of coffee, cotton, sisal, rubber and other commodities. Dar es Salaam was little but a military camp. An influenza epidemic on a nation-wide scale claimed 100,000 Africans.

The country then became a mandated territory under the fledgling League of Nations, and Britain was assigned to administer it in co-operation with friendly chiefs, British settlers, Greek business-men, and administrative officers from London.

The deportation of large numbers of German colonizers provided a bonanza for some 10,000 Asians – India had supplied the Allies with troops – who replaced the banished German traders in towns and rural districts as *duka wallahas* (owners of small stores supplying Africans with anything from sewing machines to plugs of tobacco).

Wealthy Indians, Boers from South Africa, Greeks and British farmers bought up deserted sisal plantations at bargain prices.

Two million acres of land were set aside for agricultural development by white settlers. Few of these accepted London's edict, in the terms of the League of Nations charge, that 'the interests of the Africans are to be considered paramount in all controversial policy issues'.

A white-dominated legislative council, with no black members, was set up as an advisory body to the Governor who ruled in the name of the British crown. Pliant chiefs were made responsible for local government while young ambitious Africans fretted for *uhuru* (independence). The youngsters were barred from attending higher education colleges for fear they would return home as political agitators and, instead, basic agricultural education or handicraft training, together with the three Rs – reading, writing and 'rithmetic – were considered more suitable for them than 'dangerous' book learning.

A barabara (main road) in the Selous. Maintaining roads and tracks in this enormous expanse is a constant challenge.

From 1928 onwards wildlife conflicted with tribal agricultural values in the then miniature Selous but, in 1930, when a severe economic depression had stunted development schemes, the bottom had drop-

39

ped out of the economy with a slump in sisal prices, and poor harvests, droughts and swarms of locusts that darkened the sun had laid the people low, there arrived in the country (Tanganyika as it was now called) another charming and slightly dotty Englishman. Like F. C. Selous, he had been a pupil at Rugby; and like Selous he had an entirely un-English name. He was to become the 'father' of the reserve as we know it today.

Constantine J. Phillip Ionides, son of a London surgeon of Greek descent, introduced salmon and pheasant poaching as an extra-mural activity while a cadet in England's prestigious Sandhurst Military Academy. He joined the King's African Rifles with the sole purpose of getting his fare paid to the still-dark continent so that he could become a white hunter. Three years of this – with between times a spot of gorilla and elephant poaching in the Belgian Congo – and he became tired of the average safari clients. 'Rich yobs with their bored, bejewelled wives,' he called them.

So, in September 1933, when Hitler was setting the Nazi cat among the settler pigeons by demanding the return to Germany of Tanganyika and the other former possessions abroad, Ionides took a job as a game ranger. (The penny-pinching British administration paid him less than a speed typist's wages – £50 a month.)

A loner, Ionides did all his game control safaris on foot, frequently covering hundreds of miles over periods of several months. In this way, he was to become a renowned naturalist and a world authority on the wide range of poisonous snakes he collected. His home in the wild, with snakeskins hanging from the rafters, was little more than a shack of mud, wood and wattle poles. Set in a sleeping-sickness belt, it was cut off for weeks in the long rains.

A flat back millipede marching as to war.

As he would rarely reveal his Christian names, except to the closest of friends, Ionides became known to the colonial whites throughout his life as 'Iodine'. He tolerated the nickname with good humour, but was secretly proud of the tag the Tanganyika tribespeople gave him – *Bwana Nyoka*, meaning 'Snake Man'.

Between stalking and shooting man-eating lions and rogue elephants, Ionides, who was a strict disciplinarian, would sometimes punish an errant African game scout with a few lashes of his rawhide whip. Nobody appeared to mind this summary punishment very much for the eccentric hermit of the *bushveld* was regarded by his men as a powerful wizard – mostly on account of his hat. This was a tattered, once wide-brimmed thing that half a century before may have belonged to a middle-European countess. By the time 'Iodine' adopted it, the hat looked like a cracked flowerpot. Because of this crazy article of headgear, and because of his prowess in the field, the superstitious Africans invested him with magic powers and held him in awe. They were certain, for instance, that he could hold long conversations with snakes, and Ionides did nothing to disabuse them of such ideas.

Tanganyika was not to become a battleground again in World War

II, but 3,000 Germans were interned at the outbreak of war in 1939. 100,000 Tanganyikans, black, white and brown, joined the British armed forces, and Ionides trekked for a week to the nearest recruiting station to re-enlist in the K.A.R.

Before the war was over, he was de-mobbed at the age of forty-one because of deafness, as a result of an eardrum shattered in action, and he went back to his solitary duties on the range in southern Tanganyika where he was to become something of a man of destiny in conservation terms.

First of all he had to tackle the most horrific outbreak of man-eating by lions ever recorded anywhere. Over a period of two years a thousand men, women and children were seized and eaten alive by eleven or twelve marauders, hunting singly or in groups.

In the midst of a disastrous drought, he had to cope with a plague of ivory poachers who had taken advantage of the fact that most of his small band of game scouts were away on war service. Ionides put down the gangs with ruthless, 'shoot-to-kill' anti-poaching sweeps.

In 1945, as World War II ended, he began to nag the colonial government to implement a grand scheme which he had drawn up ten years earlier. This was to make the Selous twenty times larger, and to carry out a mass removal of villagers from all the tribal settlements within the territory he envisaged. He was helped to some degree in this campaign by the fact that parts of this area had been gazetted by the colonial government in the thirties – not, however, for wildlife conservation areas but merely as regions into which crop-raiding elephants, rounded up in control operations, could be driven.

Bwana Nyoka put up a powerful case for the creation of a huge wild animal reserve completely free from human rights but it is unlikely that he would have achieved his revolutionary aim in the face of stonewall official attitudes, were it not for a series of sleeping-sickness epidemics that provided the impetus for the compulsory evacuation of all humans from thousands of square miles. The authorities ensured there would be no re-occupation simply by declaring the 'no-man's land' both a game reserve and a deadly disease area. The abject failure of the British government's grandiose scheme for the mass cultivation of groundnuts in the vicinity to produce post-war supplies of oil, also helped the decision along.

A thousand Wangindo hunters and honey collectors (who used to raid each other's villages in the old days for children to barter for flintlocks, gunpowder and salt with Arab slave traders) were particularly bitter about losing their homeland. To this day, they believe the enforced exodus was but an excuse to provide a rich hunting ground for the white man – and to some degree this has become true.

The Haya people, on the other hand, protested that they had long-term squatters' rights in the Selous; and they had a very valid point. They claimed – and their assertion is now backed by a couple of American scientists – that between 1,500 and 2,000 years ago their ancestors (so-called 'primitives'), were producing medium carbon

OVERLEAF: *A pride of lion seeks the shade of a tree in the northern Selous.*

41

steel in pre-heated, forced-draught furnaces, technologically more advanced than any in use in Europe until the middle of the nineteenth century. (The remains of rough kilns, buckskin bellows and lengths of clay piping have, in fact, been discovered on a hill at Furu in the Ruaha district of the reserve, testifying to a complex African Iron Age.)

The traditional Haya furnace, worked by the black smelters long ago, is cone-shaped, five feet high, made of slag and mud, and built over a pit packed with partially burned swamp reeds. These charred grasses provided the carbon that combined with molten iron ore to produce steel. Several ceramic blowpipes extended into the furnace chamber near the base, each connected to a hide bellows that forced pre-heated air into the charcoal-fuelled furnace. Achieving temperatures higher than 1,800 degrees Centigrade, the Haya of that previously unknown African civilization were able to produce their carbon steel for weapons and ornaments.

The British case for driving out the Selous people was far stronger in respect of the livestock-owning tribes. The guardian of the natural sanctity of the Selous is no longer than the nail of a little finger – the scissor-winged tsetse fly that kills off cattle wholesale with the *trypanosomiasis* (sleeping sickness) it carries. As an African's herds are his wealth, the fly makes human habitation in this case impractical, to say the least. The tsetse, with a silent approach and a sting like the jab of a red-hot needle, is no threat to wild animals who are, in general, immune from its attacks; and, happily, there has been no human case of sleeping sickness in the Selous for nearly thirty years. However, the robust fly can be a torment to travellers there.

By the time Ionides, now a senior game ranger, had achieved his goal, African preoccupation with Tanganyikan independence had increased sharply, and inter-tribal rivalries were over-ridden by a powerful national spirit. As the League of Nations had ceased to exist and had been replaced by the United Nations, the country was a U.N. Trust Territory and Britain was charged with developing it towards *uhuru* (independence).

By 1951, the Selous, with a few important exceptions, had taken on the form in which it now exists. At that time Ionides gained a valuable assistant, a gaunt young man called Brian Nicholson. Born in Kenya, he was like Ionides in many ways: dedicated, determined and with a reserved, introverted temperament. They were ideally matched. Operating the reserve with the minimum of funds, the couple worked so closely and effectively together that the Africans thought they were father and son.

On foot safaris, lasting maybe two or three weeks, they would be map-making one day (the only available maps of the area were based on sketchy German surveys) and on the next, fighting poachers who carried guns and spears tipped with deadly poison. Between times they set up game control posts, or might be seen collecting flora that was important either to the diet of animals or in comparing varying

A flowering branch of the Byrsocarpus *species, a low tree fairly common in coastal and riverine forest.*

types of habitat. They carried beans, maize-meal and salt for themselves and their porters, supplemented by game meat, fish and whatever honey they could find on the march.

When *Bwana Nyoka* left the Tanganyika Game Department in 1955, Nicholson carried on the man's unrelenting fight with the British government to obtain ecologically vital additions to the Selous. Thirteen years later he was to bury Ionides' ashes in a copper urn in the heart of the reserve on Nandanga mountain after Ionides had died in Nairobi Hospital.

45

As young Nicholson began his poorly-paid duties and uphill tasks alone, African ex-servicemen and scholars were forming the country's first black political party – the Tanganyika African National Union (T.A.N.U.). From it emerged Julius Kambarage Nyerere, goatherd son of a minor chief's eighteenth wife, who was to lead his country to freedom and become generally known as *Mwalimu*, the Teacher. British civil servants, meanwhile, continued to look down their noses at the efforts of Nicholson and another dedicated expatriate, Allen Rees, who joined him in 1957. Rees was the epitome of the clean-limbed, goodlooking young Englishman and now, many years later, he is following the sun around the world in his yacht, *Fidiya*, which is built of Tanzanian timber.

'From the earliest days of the British tenancy there never was any official policy directed towards the development of game reserves,' says Nicholson, now a bush pilot based in Nairobi. 'There were simply areas set aside for the maintenance of wildlife, and the idea that they could play an important part in the economy of the country was never seriously considered. This goes a long way to explain the negative attitude that was adopted by the colonial administration towards us.

A young lion blends with the subtle tones of the dry season grasses of the Selous.

'With a few notable exceptions, most officers in government service looked upon game as a problem – either to cattle or cultivation – and game reserves as useless tracts of land which could not be used for anything else. Game rangers were cranks to be tolerated, and the Game Department was a sort of Cinderella which was grudgingly allocated inadequate funds and staff to be used mainly on game control work.

'The picture started to change when the impact of tourism began to assume increasing importance to the (British-ruled) East African territories of Tanganyika, Kenya and Uganda, and it was apparent from the start that East Africa's unique wildlife was the main attraction.

'With the development of national parks and growing local and international interest in these animals, the Tanganyika Game Department began to expand and exert more influence. As a result, the staff and financial problems became easier and our proposals for protecting and utilising wildlife were taken seriously at high levels of government.

'By 1958 it was clear that Tanganyika was moving towards independence, and the need to establish a foundation for an economically self-supporting state undoubtedly had its effect on promoting tourism and, through this, the development of wildlife.

'In practice, the national parks got the lion's share of funds and publicity, but we in the Selous benefited increasingly.'

With *uhuru* in sight, the Anglo-American Corporation began searching for minerals in the Selous (nothing has since been heard of this survey), and among the ground prospectors was South African-born Terry Irwin. He gave up this back-breaking job after nine months to join Nicholson and Rees as a £60-a-month game ranger.

'We were paid like beggars, but felt like kings,' says the stocky, ebullient Irwin. 'I'd have, say, fifty or more porters on safari – with porters to carry the other porters' food and belongings! We had to walk everywhere. There was very little alternative, especially during the rains when entire tracks were washed away.'

Brian Nicholson, Allen Rees and Terry Irwin spent much of their time shooting elephants that had strayed out of the Selous and were destroying *shambas* (the maize fields of small farmers), or cornering and destroying lions who had adopted the habit of devouring passers-by. The three men hunted down 'Lion Men', black members of a dreaded voodo sect who donned lion skins to attack and kill their victims.

The trio were still at their perilous and exacting tasks, overworked and underpaid when, at midnight on 8 December 1961, a Tanganyikan army officer lit a torch of freedom in a snowstorm on the summit of Mount Kilimanjaro.

In a crowded sports stadium in Dar, the Union Jack was hauled down a flagpole. In the glare of a searchlight, amid a roar of cheers, a green, black and golden-yellow flag was hoisted in its place. Mainland

A handsome male lion leaving adolescence for full-maned grandeur stretches luxuriously in the bush.

On a fragment of dried bark a veined swallowtail butterfly (Graphium leonidas) *spreads its wings.*

Tanganyika – soon to become Tanzania in a union with the offshore clove islands of Zanzibar – was an independent state. A few hours later, in a morning ceremony of pomp and pageantry, Prince Philip, representing Queen Elizabeth II, handed Nyerere, the country's first president, the parchment 'instruments' of sovereignty.

Julius Nyerere, a far-sighted and practical intellectual, whose hobby was translating the works of Shakespeare into Swahili, was one of the first leaders of the new-born black nations of the era to proclaim protection for wild animals.

'We solemnly declare we will do everything in our power to ensure that our children's grandchildren will be able to enjoy this rich and precious inheritance,' he pledged. 'These creatures are important not only as a source of wonder and inspiration but are an integral part of our natural resources, and of our future livelihood and well-being.'

But a few village headmen saw things in a somewhat different light. Chiefs whose people had always regarded wild creatures as *nyama* or 'meat on the hoof' wanted all elephants killed. They argued, strangely, that there were no elephants roaming London, New York or other modern centres of the world and therefore it was 'uncivilized' to keep them.

But President Nyerere was as good as his word. It became the policy of the government to develop wildlife as a national asset. There were early moves to strengthen the Game Division and to ease the problems facing it and, to that end, the president directed that there should be no lack of funds for field work.

A centre to train African personnel to man the game sanctuaries was established on a national basis, and the Selous remained inviolate. It was allowed to grow even larger to provide a source of income from visiting hunting parties and, while Nyerere's black government saw the Selous as a valuable resource in its own right, its name remained unchanged.

This last fact is remarkable because, in the eyes of some Africans, F. C. Selous epitomized the colonial raj which came to African chiefly to decimate the game. The Africans argue that their own people merely killed from hunger or to protect their crops, not from 'a mere urge to create carnage and destruction'. But the Tanzanian government, despite having 'Africanized' many aspects of life in the country (such as the names of streets and buildings) out of national pride, does not appear to share this view, and the reserve continues to be 'The Selous'.

The reserve then produced a first-generation of outstanding black wardens – men who were free to act, improvise and reform on their own initiative. It was no easy task for these people who ushered in the post-independence years of the reserve because, apart from braving malaria, dysentery and other tropical diseases, they had to face the hostility of a number of their own people who, with the white man no longer boss, were unable to understand why the Selous could not be thrown open to them and their families for settlement.

5. Elephant Kingdom

IT SEEMS IRONIC that the swashbuckling Selous, the greatest elephant killer of his time, is buried alone surrounded by the largest single host of the African mammoths known to man.

A brilliant young British scientist, Iain Douglas-Hamilton, first cousin of the 15th Duke of Hamilton and the Earl of Selkirk, has counted them in the reserve; and thinks his own figure of 120,000 may be on the low side. East Africa is still rich in colourful characters and, at thirty-eight, Iain (author with his attractive wife, Oria, of the bestseller *Among The Elephants*) is one of them.

Able to trace his aristocratic ancestry back to the Premier Peer of Scotland and Keeper of the Palace of Holyrood, Iain has a well-deserved reputation as one of the world's leading authorities on elephant behaviour.

In 1963, during a summer vacation at Oxford University where he was studying zoology, he came to Tanzania, having been invited to be an assistant in an animal research project on the Serengeti plains.

'I had wanted to work with animals in Africa ever since I can remember,' he says. 'As a child, I read of vast horizons in little-explored lands ... places like the Selous and Serengeti. Adventures with wild beasts and hair's breadth escapes of tough resourceful men like Selous, who survived by their bushcraft, fascinated me.'

Before he took on the great elephant census in the Selous, Iain lived for five years among 450 elephants in Tanzania's Lake Manyara national park and was awarded a doctorate for his outstanding research work there. This greatest-ever census was the first of a series of continent-wide elephant counts for the International Union for the Conservation of Nature (I.U.C.N.), the World Wildlife Fund, and the New York Zoological Society.

Charming and resourceful (he has survived a rhino stepping on him by rolling out from under the bad-tempered beast), Dr Douglas-Hamilton looks the part of the safari scientist. His blond hair is generally tousled, and he has that faint air of distraction common to his kind. He normally wears in both town and country a well-used pair of khaki shorts, tennis shoes or sandals, and a faded blue, open-neck shirt.

An elephant browses among the grasses and dwarf palms of northern Selous.

51

This mild appearance is deceptive. He is as much a daredevil as his cousin, the Duke, whose hobbies are listed in Debrett's Peerage as motor racing, skin-diving and ski-ing. Although his family has a history of tragic flying accidents, Iain learned to fly a plane some years ago, and he has become a skilful and daring bush pilot as part of his scientific work. Now he can just about land his plane on a pound note.

While he finds the Selous a heartening exception, Iain's grave fear is that more than half the elephant population in the rest of Africa may become extinct within the next ten years. To him elephant epitomize the wilderness, and he is grateful that there are still some unspoilt elephant ranges remaining like the Selous where, as he does constantly, one can walk up close to an elephant on foot.

'But to discover such places you have to search and search hard for you will seldom find them in the guide books. You'll need to be self-sufficient and adventurous; then you may find the true wilderness.

'As the explorer Baker of the Nile remarked in 1896: "Being charged by an elephant is a new sensation – very absorbing for the time – and would be an excellent relaxation once a week for over-worked men in high office."'

Elephants need space, Iain says, and in Africa they wander from deserts to dripping dank forests, and from mountain slopes down to sea level.

Combretum constrictum: a widespread genus of African trees and creepers whose flowers are various hues of pink or red.

'On the surveys I fly in Africa, all too often I come across miles of harsh landscape where, until a few years ago, elephant thrived along the water-courses. Now I may find bones, a skull or two, sometimes a corpse held together in its dried-up skin like a mummy. Often these spread-out carcases are the only signs left of elephants.

'To find ways of preserving the elephants and their wilderness presents man with more problems and paradoxes than any other animal. Of all the wild animals, elephants interact with man the most, whether as raiders of crops, destroyers of woodlands, earners of tourist revenues, or providers of ivory, and there is always lively debate over how they should be preserved, conserved, hunted or managed.'

After weighing thousands of African elephant tusks, Dr Douglas-Hamilton found that an average pair turns the scale at about twenty-seven pounds, which means that a ton of ivory is equivalent to roughly a hundred elephants.

'Official ivory exports from Africa are often as much as fifty per cent lower than the true total,' says Iain. 'Price rises have given profiteers the means of bribing and smuggling on a scale which is only exceeded by the international traffic in drugs.'

Within one year, imports of ivory at a Far East port rose forty per cent – from 515 tons to 710 tons – and Customs officials discovered ivory being shipped disguised as machinery. Ivory leaving Africa in a single year, Iain calculates, may have come from anything between 100,000 and 400,000 elephants. He has developed a network of informants across the African continent: fellow scientists, game wardens, hunters and farmers act as early warning systems to tell him of elephants in danger of extinction.

'Elephants face three threats to their survival. The first is straight-forward human predation, mainly for ivory but also in defence of crops. The second threat is loss of range associated with a rising human population, an inevitable process which can only end when the human population is controlled. The third threat is the habitat degradation within the elephant sanctuaries, caused as a direct consequence of compression.'

Dr Douglas-Hamilton sees the continental picture as one of marked decline: 'The northernmost elephants live in Mauritania, but not one has been seen in the last ten years – only their droppings indicate their existence. In Chad it is reported that rockets have been used to shoot at elephants from helicopters. In the Ivory Coast, a Minister re-marked that unless draconian measures were taken to curb the poaching, the country would have to change its name.

'From the Sudan I have received reports that some tribes are still burning elephants to death by setting alight the long grass around a herd. Even if the elephants escape the flames, their feet become charred as they walk over red-hot ashes, and lame elephants are an easy target for spears.

'Kenya has lost more than half her elephants since 1970. Some have died due to drought, but the major cause has been ivory poaching. Uganda has shown an even greater decline, and within the Kabalega national park itself, elephant numbers crashed from 14,000 to just a handful. In West Africa, in countries such as Ghana, Liberia and Sierre Leone, the elephants are hunted for their meat rather than their ivory because human density and protein deficiency are much higher there than elsewhere.'

Out of the thirty-four countries in Africa that still have elephants, the populations are probably declining in all but four. One of these is little Rwanda, one of the poorest countries in the world, where most of the land is needed for growing crops. As a result of intense pressure from the people who live there, all but twenty-six of their elephants have been eliminated in a shooting programme. The remaining elephants are now in a reserve. The other countries are Botswana and South Africa, where most of the elephants were exterminated over a hundred years ago but where the remnants are now strictly protected, and Tanzania, where there are probably 300,000 elephants.

'In Tanzania, where there are huge wildernesses with the largest concentrations of wildlife anywhere in the world, policies of conserva-tion are actively propagated throughout the ranks of political leader-ship and right down to the grass-roots.'

Iain feels that the way people think of elephants may be vital to the animals' survival: 'For instance, on the shores of Lake Chad there's a tribe who don't kill elephants because they believe they are descended from them. In Ethiopia, the elephant was held to be the most holy of all animals because of its sexual moderation. It is frequently depicted

LEFT: *Leaden skies over the swelling Rufiji river.*

ABOVE: *Tears of rain glisten on leafless fronds.*

ABOVE RIGHT: *Annual long and heavy rains fill the rivers and flood the land.*

RIGHT: *Elephant family groups water at evening on the shores of Lake Nahato.*

LEFT: *An impala nibbles the first grass, a green carpet laid overnight by seasonal rains.*

in the country's ancient rock churches. The Ethiopian knew the art of elephant training in the Middle Ages, and it may have come to them from the people of the even older African civilization of Kush, who are said to have trained elephants for war as early as 800 B.C. – long before Ptolemies used African elephants in Egypt or Hannibal marched his African elephants over the Alps to strike at Rome. Sadly, there are only remnant elephant populations left in Ethiopia.'

Iain's I.U.C.N. brief that led him in the first instance to the Selous is to make a precise, science-based calculation of the overall status of the elephant in Africa. The most important questions he has to answer are:

Which specific areas, from which countries, are losing elephants, and why?

How precisely does the mortality divide between poaching and other causes such as drought, range depletion, over-concentration in national parks, and natural die-off?

What are the trends in elephant birth-rate?

What are the precise mechanics of the ivory trade, country by country?

How do the authorities in individual countries calculate the economic value of an elephant – in terms of meat and ivory profit to private enterprise, or as a self-sustaining, resource-producing, continuous income to national exchequers through tourism?

Is there any official appreciation anywhere in Africa of the elephants' value in the vaguer terms of aesthetics, culture, science, pride, prestige and heritage in trust?

The basic objective of this long, novel project is 'to assess the current status and future prospects of the African elephant, and to recommend an action programme to I.U.C.N./W.W.F. for improving the conservation of these species'. The ultimate goal will be to encourage people and governments to value elephants both for their intrinsic value and for their economic potential as a self-sustaining natural resource.

Iain Douglas-Hamilton began his Selous census with the distribution of a questionnaire to official and private sources in order to delineate current elephant ranges, define initial population estimates, and determine the main trends in elephant population dynamics. Then he and Oria went on a 'recce' in the Selous. The couple covered a good deal of ground, motoring and on foot, as they sought out elephants congregated in the trees and on the hillsides.

'It was tough tiring work in a torrid January week,' Iain told me. 'One lake we came across looked so inviting we stripped and dived in. We had rowed out in a dinghy to a small island in the centre of the lake. Someone told us there were no crocs. I saw hundreds in there from the air later on.'

He regards the Selous as an area of key importance in understanding elephant biology throughout Africa, and on that preliminary

Bright white sand lies on the bed of a river in September, the dry season.

56

reconnaissance with his wife he was able to familiarize himself with the reserve and its problems.

His first – wet season – count was carried out soon afterwards, over a period of five weeks. For four or five hours a day continuously, he flew his red and white four-seater aircraft *Bravo Alpha Delta* with its elephant insignia on the fuselage. The plane was fitted with a radar altimeter which he says was essential for height control – 'essential' indeed, for most of the time Iain flew *Bravo Alpha* at a mere 250 feet, skirting the mountains and almost brushing the tops of the acacias.

In his cool and sober language, this risky process – with little hope of being found alive if he crashed – was 'the most logical and efficient way to employ the aircraft, flying regularly-spaced transects so that data on numbers, distribution and habitat could be collected simultaneously'.

With a colleague of Iain's in the right-hand front seat of the plane, two specially trained African observers from the Tanzanian Game Department occupied the rear seats.

'We had tested these chaps for aptitude and accuracy in crash-course sessions. They had to count animals in groups – we intended to make a note of all large creatures as well as elephant – on slides flashed on a screen for five seconds.'

These observers scanned strips of ground demarcated by parallel white streamers attached to the struts on either side of the aircraft. 'All elephant seen within the streamers were counted and the results dictated into tape-recorders so that the observers didn't have to take their eyes off the ground.' The transects were five nautical miles square, and the overall grid covered the entire reserve. All the while, Iain's companion was taking pictures to build up a photographic library of every major habitat in the Selous.

Funded by the African Wildlife Leadership Foundation of Washington, D.C., the second – dry season – census was undertaken in the months of August and September. The white ribbons on the struts were replaced with sections of big game fishing rods.

'Fewer hours were flown since we were familiar with the ground and were able to eliminate dead time. In three areas, we sampled the age structure of the elephant populations by vertical aerial photography.'

In a dry season sunset zebra appear to move across the plain with flame at their feet.

As before, daily summaries were made of each transect flown, with totals for every species recorded in each cell of the particular grid. The distribution maps made from these statistics look like giant crossword puzzles.

His second count showed little change in the distribution of elephant except in the eastern Selous where he found they had left the sun-scorched plains to occupy the thickets on the hills for both food and shade.

'We sighted poachers' camps on both counts, and found most elephant carcasses were concentrated in the more accessible northern end of the reserve. [Observations from helicopters over the Selous have shown game authorities that they could recover £500 worth of ivory *an hour* from natural mortality rates alone.]

'Poaching in the Selous, however, is low compared to other parts of Africa. In Tsavo national park in Kenya, for instance, there were more dead elephants to be found than live – a ratio of 103/100.'

Visibility was far better on the second tally since the long grass was mainly burnt and the trees had lost their leaves, leaving a mesh of branches through which elephant were clearly visible. Iain says: 'In consequence, our estimates were higher, although we don't claim more than ninety-five per cent accuracy on such counts. We have to take into consideration observer under-count, caused by poor visibility. We miss quite a few jumbo under the trees in both the wet and dry seasons.'

He envisages the day when he may be using new counting techniques such as radio tracking from satellites to determine the forest ranges of elephant, or monitoring them deep in the jungles with infra-red sensing techniques.

'Then all our figures should be right on – down to the newest calf struggling to its feet in the undergrowth.'

Iain sees the Selous as 'a priceless asset whose true magnitude is becoming evident for the first time'. He is eagerly anticipating the day he will return there 'with a few space-age gadgets', to make that pin-sharp inventory of all its animal wonders.

6. Flying Squirrels

EVERY YEAR WHEN the tall spreading marula trees are in fruit the Selous elephants go on a binge.

Groping among the branches with their trunks, entire families tear down what look like plums, ranging in colour from pale green to yellow. They have a tart-sweet taste which the animals love, and they feast on each tree until it is stripped of its bounty. Then the elephants go off to the nearest waterhole to drink their fill, and the trouble begins.

Late in the evening an elephant stands silhouetted amid palms on the banks of the Rufiji river.

Nyasa white-faced wildebeest, which range only south of the Rufiji river.

The marula plums, rich in vitamin C, ferment in their stomachs. The more water they drink, the drunker they become – reeling cross-eyed from one tree to another, trumpeting boozily. Africans make a powerful brew from the plum (it belongs to the mango family), and the elephants' monumental hangovers have been known to last for a couple of days or more!

Elephant may be almost as numerous as flying ants in the wildlife refuge of the Selous, but it is also the home of hosts of rare, strange or exotic creatures.

High on the list is the grotesque aardvark (pronounced 'ard-vark') or African ant-bear. (The name, however, is of Boer origin and means 'earth pig'.) With its serpent-like tongue, tubular snout, long pointed ears and strong kangaroo-type tail, the aardvark – often covered in reddish-brown soil – seems more like a science fiction horror encountered in a nightmare. A mixture of wild and domestic animal, it has a large body, an arched spine and the powerful claws of a bear with which it digs into termite hills at a remarkable speed. The younger animals are covered with a thick coat of bristly yellow hairs like a pig, but in adults these hairs become sparse and take on a dull grey, earthy hue.

The aardvark feeds at night on ants and termites and is rarely seen by day. I detected its spoor throughout the open country and light forest areas of the reserve. During the day, the aardvark hides in a burrow that has been dug deep in the sand or soft earth by its claws at a furious rate. It can disappear in a matter of seconds while making one of these underground homes.

The ordinary wildebeest, or brindled gnu; their range is to the north of the Rufiji.

Driving along tracks at night, particularly during rainstorms when

the white ants on which the animals prey are more active, the headlights of our safari vehicle would sometimes reveal an ant-bear making off at a clumsy, bouncing gallop with its donkey-ears cocked and tail stretched out behind. One hard-drinking visitor, it is said, became an instant teetotaller on seeing one of these creatures gallumphing towards him.

The aardvark's burrow may be a simple hole with a single entrance, or a complicated maze of galleries spread over a wide area; snakes, warthogs and owls breed, or lie up, in abandoned ant-bear holes. A single aardvark 'cub' is born in the burrow at a time, and the youngster accompanies its mother on ant-hunting expeditions until it has learned to forage for itself. The adult male of the species lives alone.

Although this weird mammal's sense of smell and hearing are acute, its sight is poor and it appears to be almost blinded by sunlight. They are active mainly during the darkest, moonless nights when, except for a passing snack of wild cucumbers, they make a meal of termites and ants. They sometimes dig out termite 'stalagmites', projecting their protractile, sticky tongues – eighteen inches long – into the passages of the pinnacle to collect several pallid termite nymphs at a time. According to some authorities, the aardvark can cover as much as ten miles overnight, going from one termite hill to another or snatching up ants from long columns marching overland.

Caught out in the open, the ant-bear makes a tasty meal for a lion, although they can run fast when frightened and are fierce fighters when cornered. Other nocturnal enemies of the aardvark are the leopard and the *unungunungu*, better known as the African porcupine, whose long black and white quills are needle-sharp and make a deep, nasty wound.

South of the Rufiji river, the Selous is one of the last refuges in the world of the white-faced Nyasaland gnu. It is already extinct – hunted and poached out – in the southern African country after which it was named (although that country is now called Malawi). It is a hump-backed antelope with cow-like horns, and derives its name from the fact that it has a broad chevron of white hair on its forehead between the horns and its beard. The creature's mane and tail are similar to those of a horse.

A member of the wildebeest family from the plains, the Nyasaland gnu is gregarious and generally lives in a herd. Like its wildebeest cousins, it has a bizarre and rather stupid appearance in the style of a Thurber moose. For all that, it is given to skittish behaviour, suddenly cantering round in circles at some silent signal, with much mane-tossing and tail whisking.

The adult gnu is courageous in defence of its spindly-legged calves which have silky fawn coats and 'moo' like domestic cows. Only lion will tackle fully grown bulls or cows. Young gnu are a common prey for lions, especially during calving in March and April, but there are several instances on record where a bull has charged and driven off an attacking lion.

Half hidden in a glade, a female greater kudu with her calf.

The grass-eating gnu is an easy target for the hunter as it is highly inquisitive. It stops to stare at any approaching strange object, or gives away its presence by snorting loudly. Then, with one accord, the herd will wheel round and gallop away. After a short distance of flight their curiosity again overcomes them, and they will stop and turn once more to gaze at the intruder.

Another rare gnu found in the Selous bears a resemblance in some features – hooves, body and tail – to the Nyasaland species. It is the sassaby; but unlike the grey wildebeest its coat is a glossy purplish-red with cresentic horns and dark patches on its upper limbs and face. Also a grazer but sometimes found sheltering in thorn-bush thickets, the graceful sassaby has the reputation of being one of the swiftest of all African antelopes. As a rule, it spends its life in family groups or in small herds of up to a dozen.

Both the blue duiker and the red duiker live within the reserve. The former is actually slate-grey, but the red duiker has a bright orange coat with blue-ish legs and a band of similar colour from nose to tail. The duiker is a small, shy antelope, and the red species inhabit dense bush, woodlands and mountain forests. Described by experts as 'very rare', the blue duiker is generally glimpsed only as a fleeting shadow.

One of the most handsome antelopes in Africa inhabits thick Selous bush. This is the white-striped greater kudu, whose bulls have long, elegantly spiralled horns. The calves are reddish in colour, the cows smaller and more slender than the male but with large, prominent ears.

The greater kudu graze and browse in small herds from six to twenty cows, calves and young bulls. A big old bull is sometimes in attendance, but generally the mature bulls live apart from the females, only joining them at breeding time. The greater kudu's call is a sharp, hoarse bark.

Naturalist, C. T. Astley Maberly, who has studied African wildlife over many years, says: 'When alarmed and cantering away at their rather rocking-horse gait, kudu curl up their bushy tails over the rump, fanning out the white, bushy underside. When galloping through very dense bush, the bulls lay their huge, unwieldy horns right back along their shoulders. Male kudu are seldom attacked unless by lions, but cows and young are attacked by leopard, cheetah and wild dogs.'

The golden-yellow puku, rare or extinct in many other parts of Africa, is also found in the reserve. It is related to the Uganda kob and is a member of the water buck and reed buck family. The female has a brownish crown, but not the short thick horns of the male. The puku is never far from water, grazing on open flats bordering rivers, lakes or swamps. It gives a low penetrating whistle when sensing danger or when attacked to warn others in the herd.

Another unique small antelope known as Sharpe's grysbok takes refuge in an aardvark's former den, or among rocks and boulders of the Selous' stony hills. A prototype of Walt Disney's Bambi, the grysbok prefers a solitary existence, except during the mating season.

Seriously threatened elsewhere in Africa (for example, the habitat of one sub-species has been severely constricted by the spread of human homes and fields on the Indian Ocean clove island of Zanzibar), the red Colobus monkey lives free in the Selous. The fur on the back of this large primate – also found among forests bordering the Tana river in Kenya – is distinctively reddish-brown, black at the shoulders.

The spectacular red colobus are arboreal and live exclusively in thick or patchy forest areas. At dusk, they swing in troops like flashes of sunset between the crowns of tall trees.

As harmless as they are beautiful, the red colobus feed at dawn and sundown almost entirely on leaves and wild vegetables, They leave the trees only to forage on the ground, and drink rainwater from hollows in the trunks. Solemn-faced, they utter shrill whistling cries in chorus as they crash through the branches, the females with babies clinging to their chests.

'Wolves' in Africa? In the Selous, certainly. There we find the aardwolf which, appropriately enough in view of its name, hides in disused aardvark burrows. The aardwolf has pointed ears, a bushy tail and a sharp black muzzle, but there its resemblance to the conventional wolf ends. A white mane along an arched back and a brown-striped shaggy coat of sandy colour show its true relations – the hyena and jackal.

The tail and heavy mane, or 'cape', of long buff hairs with black tips are 'blown up' when the animal is frightened, giving a formidable appearance of almost double its size. At the same time, like the zorilla or striped polecat, it emits a vile-smelling liquid from its glands.

Called *fisi ndogo* by the Africans in Swahili, the aardwolf roams the sand-plains and thorn-scrub country. Often confused with the striped hyena, it is nocturnal and timid and few people have seen it in daylight because families or packs usually lie up in underground chambers. Several females may raise their young together in a domestic commune.

Like the aardvark, these 'wolves' live on white ants, but they have also been seen to snatch small rodents, beetles, and chicks or eggs from ground-nesting birds. Unlike the true wolf, the comparatively mild aardwolf has small teeth and a weak jaw.

As the sun sinks, there is a deep, solemn hush in the Selous forests, broken only by weird chitterings from dark forms flitting from tree to tree in the gloom. The scaly-tailed flying squirrels have begun their nightly hunt for palm nuts, berries, tender young leaves and grass shoots.

These large squirrels, the *anomaluridae*, to give them their scientific name, belong to a peculiar group of rodents now extinct except in tropical Africa. They are slenderly built and have a bushy tail on the underside of which, near where it joins the body, are two rows of sharp pointed scales directed backwards.

A hyena gnaws a piece of carcase closely watched by a vulture. A second vulture arrives to join the waiting game. The birds bicker to no purpose for soon the hyena will lope off keeping a close grip on its prize.

The squirrel's most distinctive feature is its gliding apparatus. A flap of dusky-furred skin is stretched along each side of the creature's body from forepaws to back paws. With the squirrel's legs outstretched, these lateral membranes act as wings, or a parachute, and the tail is used as a rudder.

The flying squirrels hide and sleep during the day in hollow trees or thick foliage. As night falls and a buttermilk full moon emerges from a cloud, they appear like a company of big bats, veering and zooming between the trees. Launching themselves from a tall limb with a vigorous push of their back legs, they can glide for as far as a hundred yards. Generally the glide angle is steep, and the squirrels swoop down to the lower trunk of a tree – landing with head up and tail down. Their tail-scales grip the trees and help to save the animals from slipping off. They then scamper up the bark in search of food.

The squirrels' 'wings' also provide camouflage when they land on branches during the day, for there is no distinctive shadow that spells 'squirrel' to tempt an enemy.

7. Walking Fish

SLUGGISH GIANT CATFISH that weigh up to two hundred pounds live in the waterways of the Selous. Some are bigger than the men who catch them for poor sport or their coarse, beef-red flesh. They can be taken, with little or no fight, on a stout rod, strong nylon line and a grapnel-hook baited with chunks of raw meat. The catfish eats anything from water insects to putrified hippo flesh. It has a rubbery, grey body and long, barbel-style whiskers.

Catfish hibernate deep in the river mud during the dry seasons, when they are even easier to catch than usual. Africans simply dig them out in their comatose state and club them to death. They consider the more tender tail meat a delicacy, particularly when it has been smoked over a wood fire.

A giant baobab diminishes with its immensity all other trees on the plain.

One night in the Selous I had a camp stew of catfish, onions and potatoes. It was soft and tasty after it had been stewed, but a subsequent meal of fried fish cutlets had a better flavour. From the white man's point of view, the catfish is no gourmet's delight nor a thing of beauty.

There is a small droll species of lungfish in the reserve known as the *kamisi*. In the dry season, when the surrounding ground is gripped by drought and resembles a parched mosaic, the *kamisi* leaves its dried-up pool and lumbers overland on its fins to another waterhole and settles down again.

It's unlikely to happen but I imagined the consternation, even horror, of a stranger coming across the combination of an aardvark, a strolling fish and a gaggle of red bats. These bats, minions of Dracula, previously unknown to science, have been discovered up a small river of the Selous.

One of the Selous' most voracious oddities stays hidden most of the time and is less than half an inch long – the lion ant. This creature feeds by moving in a circle in the sand beneath a tree until it has made a small pit in the soil. Then it waits patiently. Other ants or bugs slip and tumble into the lion ant's lair where he waits with deadly mandibles poised.

A chameleon is grotesque in close-up. Allen Rees.

But woe betide the lion ant if he is caught outside his den in the path of a column of *siafu*, or soldier ants, that devour every living

69

LEFT: *Starkly dominant in a small grove of trees near Beho Beho is the* Sterculia appendiculata.

RIGHT: *Tangles of forest and woodland in the Selous are described by the African word* miombo. *As the seasons change and the rains start, pause and stop there occurs on a single branch an artist's palette of* miombo *colours.*

A raging fire cruelly chars trees and land. Most fires are lit by hunters to open up their view.

thing they encounter. They stream through forest and bush – broad, quivering bands of black – guarded on both flanks by merciless soldiers with large waving pincers. When a column leaves its bivouacs and fans out, there is a wholesale killing of other ants, spiders, cockroaches, caterpillars, grasshoppers and even small snakes and lizards.

One of the few creatures which is comparatively safe from the soldier ants is a giant millipede known as Tanganyika Train or *chongalolo* that has what look like a million reddish-brown legs and a glossy black shell.

Still in the insect world, the praying mantis of the Selous shows a chameleon-like adaptation to the colour of its immediate surroundings. Allen Rees says that on mauve flowers they are mauve, and so on, while in spots where there have been bush fires they take on the colours of charred leaves.

A small, yellow-and-black reed frog Rees collected upstream in a tributary of the Rufiji, has not yet been named by scientists.

Even the common tree frogs are fascinating. When the Selous' dry season changes overnight and the annual rains begin, the frogs appear from their burrows deep in the earth to mate by the nearest stretch of water. Clinging to trees, they watch as, in the rain, their tapioca-like spawn turns to tadpoles in the pools.

71

Thick smoke hovers over a blackened landscape. At the end of the '70s, official thinking in the reserve was to study the effect of burning on small areas only.

Among the bizarre arboreal sights of the Selous is the monkey bread tree, or baobab, silhouetted on the skyline, looking like something hideous out of a Grimm's Fairy Tale. One of the largest (in girth) and oldest trees in the world, the baobab is said to live up to 2,000 years. It thrives at low levels in hot muggy climates. Dr David Livingstone, the explorer, referred to it as 'a carrot planted upside down'. Africans believe it was uprooted by the devil and pushed back into the ground with its roots in the air.

This strange tree has been worshipped by tribespeople for hundreds of years as a fertility symbol. Parts of it are used for soap, necklaces, glue, cloth (from the fibres), and *dawa* (medicine). The pulp in its maraca-shaped 'fruit' tastes like cream of tartar, and is used in native beer. In times of severe drought, elephant will strip the trunk of a baobab and bore into the heart of the tree which stores water.

In the early morning light, its trunk and root-like branches take on a silver sheen. This turns to glowing copper in the last rays of the sun in the evening.

All over the reserve can be seen other big untidy trees with what look like German sausages dangling in the foliage. They are, in fact, known as sausage trees, or *muratina* in Swahili. Although they look appetizing enough at a distance, the large grey fruits are not edible, but baked they are used in the preparation of a mead-style beer. The harsh insides of the 'sausages' are sometimes used as scouring pads, or boiled down as a cure-all in African herbal medicines. The 'sausages' develop in profusion from port wine-coloured flowers that bloom at night and emit an unpleasant musty odour before they die and drop in the morning from their long, stringy stems.

72

The *mtomondo* tree which grows along the banks of rivers near the sea is the fisherman's friend because its fruit contains seeds that can be pounded to powder between stones by the game scouts, and tossed into the river as a drug to tranquillize fish. The fish then float to the surface of the water and are easily caught by hand from the bank or a boat. The *mtomondo* has fragrant white blooms with a mass of delicate tendrils which open at night.

Torrential rains – in some parts of the reserve three inches have been recorded in six hours – begin each year in a summer that is a turnabout of its equivalent in the northern hemisphere. They transform the parched bushland into vast grassy carpets on which the 'miracle of the *miombo*' (deciduous woodland) that covers more than three-fifths of the reserve, is wrought.

Swept by awesome bush fires in a dry season that is the equivalent of a western autumn (when tens of thousands of acres of waist-high grass are set ablaze by the sun's rays, bolts of tropical lightning, game scouts burning off the tall old grass to obtain fresh grazing, or by hunters to provide clear views of the quarry for their clients), the *miombo* is reduced to blackened, leafless twigs and grey ash – a 'silver death', the Africans have named it.

But the tough deep roots are not destroyed by holocausts that turn the night into a hell of flame and smoke, and under the first showers of rain from a glowering sky the gnarled bushes and stunted trees that have been dead for several weeks sprout tender new leaves; and some bushes bear creamy-white or crimson blooms. There is a spontaneous symphony of vivid green the length and breadth of the Selous: a veritable garden in Eden.

As the dry season approaches once more, the *miombo* turns to autumnal colours from gold through copper, orange and russet to rich brown, all reminiscent of an English parkland. The 'miracle' is about to begin all over again.

8. And 'Talking' Birds

It SEEMED QUITE the wrong place to bicker and quarrel. There was not a soul in sight, but the air around a clump of bushes by a trickling stream was filled with the sounds of hysterical, heated argument.

The culprits shattering the early morning peace of this remote woodland setting in the Selous with their abrasive nattering were scores of greyish-brown, speckled birds – no bigger than a garden thrush – with scaly legs and white arrowhead-shaped tips to their feathers. Their chief characteristic, according to a leading East African ornithologist, is 'a constant babbling chatter like the bandying of filthy language in a harsh voice'.

This noisy bird is – of course – the arrow-marked babbler which (with its relative the rufous chatterer that punctuates its babbling with plaintive whistles) is one of the reserve's 350 *known* feathered species. The 'filthy language' goes on without a break while the babblers are sweeping the ground, generally in thorn-bush country, for bugs and beetles. Although it seems they are swearing at their greedy companions in the flock as they fight for insects or are complaining about the scarcity of food, these are merely the social contact sounds of the group.

While the Selous is a fabulous haven of all game, it is also an immense 'aviary' of wild birds that are gorgeous, bizarre or spectacular according to a wide range of ecological conditions and habitats. And many species there are still to be discovered by science.

Everyone, however, knows vultures are part and parcel of the African bush, and both the griffin and white-backed vulture of the clan belong to the Selous. With their long wings and short tails, the vultures are as graceful in flight as they are hideous on the ground. In the air, they use rising currents of hot air (thermals) to glide and soar for hour after hour, scanning the ground with incredibly sharp eyes for signs of carrion. Once a vulture spots a dead or dying creature, it will start to glide down and is soon joined in a narrowing encircling flight by others. In this way, they pinpoint the location of a kill for tourists on safari, or show game wardens where poachers have struck.

Once they have landed beside the remains of a lion's meal or the rotting carcase of some animal that has died of disease, the soaring-

A great white egret stands in the shallows of the Rufiji, quite unconcerned by the proximity of a gleaming crocodile. Clearly they live in harmony.

eagle image of the vulture changes immediately. With their relatively small heads (naked or down-covered), evil, beady eyes and razor-sharp beaks they hiss and peck at each other while they gorge themselves on the meat. Repulsive as they are at close range, vultures are the sanitary squads of the savannah – leaving only a scattering of white bones after their feasts.

The white-backed vulture is distinguished by its conspicuous white rump, and the griffin by its scaly or spotted appearance. Both produce deep-throated croaks when squabbling over carrion.

Far more endearing but equally out of focus is the large, black and white trumpeter hornbill which is the old world equivalent of the new world toucan. Conspicuous in hot, acacia country, the hornbill has a beak out of all proportion to its size and gives loud braying cries like a donkey. It looks as though it might be protesting about the size of its bill, used primarily for feeding on fruit and berries, but this is, in fact, quite light, consisting chiefly of a honeycomb of air-cells.

On top of all this, the hornbill is considered remarkable on account of its breeding habits. At the start of the breeding season, the female climbs into a hole in a tree and mud is brought to her by the male in his huge beak. Using this and her own faeces as a sealant, the female walls up the entrance hole, leaving only a slit through which she can be fed grubs and insects by the male. During the next few weeks, the eggs are laid and hatched inside the tree-trunk prison and the female

A familiar African image: five vultures sit like sisters of doom while a sixth demonstrates that in flight the gross becomes pure grace.

The grey hornbill – memorably known by local Africans as the kolikoli.

breaks out to join the male and help him feed their young, who remain in the nest and seal it with their own faeces. The hornbills mate for life.

The trumpeter's less active relative is the ground hornbill which looks like a deformed turkey and can rarely get itself off the ground where, as it is carnivorous, it feeds on small snakes and lizards.

A look-alike, without the bill, is the noble kori bustard with three-toed feet, a long neck, brown-and-white plumage and a speckled chest. The male of the species may be five feet tall and, seemingly unafraid of humans, he struts in a stately manner over open grassland in search of all types of insects.

Still out on the plains, we encounter now and then a long-legged grey bird with crest feathers that give the appearance of a quill pen behind one ear. Appropriately named the secretary bird, it lives on snakes, small mammals, lizards, frogs, grasshoppers and the young of ground-nesting birds, all of which it snatches up as it stalks through the grass. It builds big nests of sticks at the tops of trees and, in the breeding season, grunts like a lion.

The smaller birds which also live on the grasslands are equally fascinating. The black and white fiscal shrike, looking like a miniature hawk with its small hooked beak, stares at the ground from some vantage point such as a bush or a rock. It is watching for the slightest movement – the stirring of a blade of grass, for instance – that might

LEFT: *Searching a small waterhole for food is a hammerkop, instantly recognisable by its distinctive profile.*

BELOW LEFT: *A Goliath heron stands in a thicket of wild flowers on the banks of the Rufiji.*

RIGHT: *A lilac-breasted roller.*

BELOW: *An open-bill stork gazes across the waterhole where egrets seem like caped ghosts.*

betray the presence of a beetle, a lizard, a grasshopper or some other insect. Then it strikes in the blinking of an eye and flies off with its prey in its beak. According to experts, in times of plenty these birds use a thorn-bush as a store, impaling insects and small rodents on the thorns. But another mystery of the wild is that the shrikes never seem to return to eat the food in their open-air 'larders'.

The broad-tailed paradise whydah, a black, sparrow-like bird with a yellow nape and belly, forages among the grasses. During the breeding season, the males develop tails three times as long as themselves – struggling up in jerky fluttering flight when courting or alarmed and then dropping back suddenly to the ground as though exhausted.

There are over fifty species of sunbirds, comparable to the humming birds of the Americas, and the Selous has its share of them – in both torrid dry open country and alpine moorlands. Small and brilliantly coloured, the hovering sunbird, its wings vibrating, uses its fine curved bill to extract nectar and insects from wild flowers and the blossoms of flowering trees.

These birds with their many hues are an introduction to the superb East African starling – bright blue and green on top with a rich orange breast and white-ringed eyes. Pert and industrious, it consumes large quantities of grubs and insects.

Another bird of the plains is the yellow-collared lovebird; this a green parrot with a reddish beak, dark brown head and a yellow breastplate and collar. A seed-eater, it generally flies in small flocks

The grouped nests of tiny weaverbirds are built in tall grass overhanging a river.

but is sometimes seen in company with the red-faced mousebird which has a 'cockade' and a long slender tail. Mousebirds as a family are endemic to Africa.

The black-rumped button quail lives in the long grass, bursting skyward from one's feet with a characteristic whirr of wings.

In the woodlands, thickets and waterless upland forests of the Selous, the common African cuckoo lays its eggs in the nests of foster-parents like others of the species elsewhere in the world, but – for reasons known only to itself – reverses the normal 'kook-koo' call and coos 'koo-kook'.

The small cardinal woodpecker, with a scarlet crown or cap that gives the bird its name, flashes among the trees while, near water, there is the red-eyed dove together with the ubiquitous and beautiful lilac-breasted roller, the bulbous dusky flycatcher, the violet-crested turaco of the arboreal lourie family and the elusive Narina's trogon with its colouring of bright reds and greens.

While these birds provide a woodland palette, the black-throated honey guide is something more than just a pretty face. It may be small, but is is also markedly intelligent. As the bird's name implies, it will guide humans to the nests of wild bees in the forests in order to feed on what is left of the honeycomb after it has been cut down. When the honey guide flits from tree to tree (peeking back every so often to make sure the source of supply is still following), it utters sharp excited cries.

Being close to the Equator, the Selous is a tropical reception area for birds migrating to avoid extremes of cold elsewhere. Among these is the dainty black-and-white avocet with a slender, upturned bill which it uses like a scythe while wading in shallow water in search of aquatic insects. According to John G. Williams, an authority on East African birds, the avocet is sometimes seen in flocks 'thousands strong'.

An Egyptian goose takes off in alarm.

Other – indigenous – inland water birds are Kittlitz's sand plovers, the painted snipe (contrary to some rules of nature in respect of men and birds, the female has brighter colours than the male and initiates courtship), and the dark-brown hammerkop with a 'hammerhead' crest. It is widely believed among Africans that anyone who harms the frog-eating hammerkop will have bad luck for the rest of his life.

The blue-breasted bee-eater lives among the reeds at the edges of marshes and rivers where a black and yellow bird of the weaver family closely related to the London sparrow builds its rough, roofed nest. This domed grass structure hangs, in colonies, from tall whippy rushes or papyrus – or far out on tree branches – to keep its eggs and chicks safe from marauding snakes and lizards.

The purple gallinule, larger than a coot or a moorhen, is also a papyrus dweller. It has long, pink legs and a bright red bill.

Fork-tailed pratincoles chase insects in large flocks over the Selous lakes where African darters swim low in the water with only their pointed heads and long slender necks showing. The Africans call them

A chicken-like francolin seeks cover among stalks of dried grass.

'snake birds' for they look like a swimming reptile. The pratincoles are larger than, but similar to, the long-tailed cormorant which, when not perched in sharp relief on a limb of a drowned tree, is diving deep to catch fish in its powerful, hook-tipped beak.

The red-knobbed coot is also a strong swimmer, feeding like the purple gallinule among the reed beds around lakes and swamps.

Hiding under the cover of reeds, rushes, sedges and other aquatic plants is the shy squacco heron with stumpy, green legs, over-shadowed by the grey goliath, the largest of East African herons, that flies with its head and neck retracted to the shoulders.

In contrast to the squacco, the long-legged lily trotter is something of a show-off, picking its way daintily over the water-lily leaves in a walk-on-water act.

The biggest and best-known of the storks is the marabou, like the vulture, ugly on the ground but beautiful in soaring flight.

To many observers the marabou, with its habit of 'sitting back' on its knees on the river bank or lakeside, its bald head, air-filled pink pouch hanging from a scrawny neck and sly, hang-dog glance, is an Edwardian roue or a raddled, septuagenarian alderman. It snaps up frogs, lizards and locusts, croaks and rattles its bill when at rest, joins vultures in a meal of carrion, and is not above raking over a city rubbish dump.

The kingfishers of the Selous are as attractive as the marabou is

Four egrets aiming for the topmost branch of a bare tree seem to demonstrate an egret's landing procedure.

Centre right, an emerald spotted wood dove tones almost completely with the dark leaf-covered ground of a forest.

repulsive. The blue-metal malachite kingfisher feeds on fish fry and dragonfly larvae, and the abundantly-crested, chestnut-chested giant kingfisher hunts among the mountain rivers and streams.

A broad range of wild ducks enjoy both fresh and brackish waters – the African pochard, the garganey and Hottentot teals, the redbill and the fulvous tree duck. Their companions afloat are the pygmy goose, with its orange-yellow bill, and the handsome Egyptian goose that sometimes lands in trees.

Birds of prey have difficulty in seeing and seizing their quarry in the long grasses during the rainy season, so they tend to breed during the dry period when the grass has withered or been burned away and small creatures like mice and lizards can be easily spotted and caught. The birds of the Selous which fall into this category are Wahlberg's eagle, often confused with the tawny eagle, the hawk eagle, and the crowned hawk eagle with its distinctive crest and whistling cry.

The large black Verreaux's eagle, a rare and imposing bird, lives among the cliffs and crags of the mountain ranges and feeds on hyrax (rock rabbits).

Tasty game birds for the hunter's pot run from the partridge-type spurfowl including the yellow-necked francolin, to sand-grouse and the helmeted, crested and vulturine species of guinea fowl.

Brownish tick birds, or ox-peckers, and snowy egrets are normally seen in association with big game – searching for parasites in hide and hair. These birds ride on the backs of elephant, rhino and buffalo. They can be an irritation, but are tolerated less for their grooming activities than the fact that they give shrill cries of warning at the approach of a hunter.

No camouflage obscures the contrasting black and white colours of the fish eagle, even in flight.

The *gymnoschizorhis personata* – named by the scientific world long ago – is a member of the turaco family and has a professorial gaze. For all its attractive green patch in the middle of a white chest, long grey tail and cinnamon-crested head, the *gymnoschizorhis* fares no better with its common name, the bare-faced go-away bird – derived from its raucous call, 'Go-away, Go-away-ay'. No wonder it gives vent to wild chuckles as it perches in a Selous euphorbia tree or flies around the bush country and woodland savannah.

At nightfall, the speckled dusky nightjar comes into its own. It is an aerial feeder, employing its big mouth and rictal bristles as a net. It feeds by catching the insects which are swept into the air by the progress of oncoming cars. The nightjar waits on the road ignoring the headlights of approaching vehicles and takes off with only a split second to spare before being crushed beneath the wheels.

Feeding on rodents, the African barn owl sometimes uses deserted hammerkop's nests in which to lay its eggs and rear chicks. Alone on a black night in a Selous wood, it is an unnerving experience to hear the 'thrum' of wings followed by a maniacal shriek and ghostly snoring. But a torch-beam shows the spectral visitation is merely a barn owl returning to its nesting place after a midnight foray for rats and mice.

Oddest of the nocturnal birds, perhaps, is the spotted eagle owl, found both on the rocky slopes and savannah country of the Selous. The bird – *bubo africanus* – has the body and plumage of an eagle but the head, with prominent ear tufts, of an owl. It has a low mournful call of 'Hoo, hoo, hoo' and a sad bewildered expression. The spotted eagle owl seems to be a rare cruel joke of nature.

9. Offbeat Safaris

The Ochna *species is common among the flowering trees and shrubs of the Selous. A vivid yellow bloom in close-up.*

THERE ARE TWO tented camps in the Selous on the northern bank of the Rufiji which are used by tourists from Britain, Europe and the United States for photographic safaris. The tourists arrive from Dar by road or take a 40-minute flight in a twin-engined charter plane.

One camp is £250,000 worth of 'instant Africa' for the well-heeled (with its cocktail bar in the branches of a baobab, insect-proof luxury tents under new thatch and an African manager) while the other is a comfortable, 'no-nonsense' affair run by an hospitable bush-wise German named Karl Jahn.

Aside from organizing Land-Rover and boat trips, and foot safaris, Karl has built a floating hide on one of the Selous lakes and a platform in a tall tree from which game and birds can be photographed at close range.

By his well-stocked bar at the riverside is a small jasmine tree with fragrant flowers, each of five white petals, that form in clusters along its branches. The ground-up bark of the tree is used by Africans to alleviate fevers and cure headaches.

'We've plenty of the usual remedies for tropical dehydration,' Karl tells new arrivals as he pours a generous tot of cane gin. 'Unfortunately, they give more headaches than they cure.'

He offers 'daily laundry free of charge', and hopes one day to be able to buy the chi-chi ropeless 'Selous' tents first used by Prince Charles and Princess Anne when they were on safari in East Africa in the early seventies. His steel-plated vehicles are fitted with roof hatches from which his paying guests, wearing the customary slouch hat with (plastic) leopard-skin band, can shoot – with still or movie cameras – the 'Big Five', namely lion, buffalo, elephant, leopard and rhino.

The Selous has been described variously by the small band of game wardens and scientists who have worked there as 'fantastic', 'weird' or 'magical'. All three words, I found, are fitting. These, for instance, are the entries in my diary for a single day out of Karl's camp in the wonderful world of the Selous:

Termite hills like ogres' castles, with the bloated queen cemented in

A single jasmine bloom (Holarrhena febrifuga). *The lovely scent of these flowering trees pervades the forest in which they grow.*

87

her royal cell. Termites, or white ants, were the first beings to establish a social organization.

Thorn bushes with blanched needles two or three inches long.

A pair of fish-eagles – their shrill cries half plaintive, half imperious – in a tree overlooking a lake that mirrors the ragged clouds in an azure sky. (Are fish-eagles, with their black wings and white shirt-fronts, disembodied head-waiters?)

Tall drowned palms, still standing where they were swamped by flood water, with tops of worn out feather dusters.

Inscription in the visitors' book of a safari camp at Beho Beho (where elephant come to drink at the bar): 'If after such a visit I may die, may my death be oft-repeated.'

A bright yellow and orange butterfly poised beside a puddle.

Elephant digging for water in a dry river, scraping away the sand with their forelegs and then using their trunks to delve. The youngsters had to wait their turn when water filled the holes.

Plump vultures lined up with military precision on a branch, watching with beady eyes a lioness who has reduced an impala to a pile of bones and gristle.

No pollution of any kind, not a brick anywhere. ('The Selous is the antithesis of the population explosion and environmental degradation,' wrote Gordon Matzke, a young American scientist who studied in the reserve.)

The flies are tough. Beaten down in the cab of the Land-Rover with a rolled-up newspaper, they come back again – and again.

A foul-smelling den of hyenas in a hillside.

Birds parade on the broad back of a hippo asleep on a sandbank.

A four-foot-long monitor lizard eating crocodiles' eggs.

Antelope rams with large harems.

Wild dogs mating. A skittish piebald female and two young males. (They hunt in packs, running down their prey – it may be a wildebeest calf or a gazelle fawn – and tearing it to pieces.)

A rhino skull, minus horn.

Clouds of what are popularly known as 'flying ants', snapped up by swallows after five minutes of rain. Only a few pairs survive the predators to form new colonies of termites.

Some peculiar, hidden bird cheeps 'Pretty bird, pretty bird' like a budgerigar.

Ladybirds of polished topaz.

A twelve-foot python sunning itself on a rock.

Hippos' snorts punctuate the maddening pervasive nuptial chorus of cicadas that have emerged in their tens of thousands after a long hibernation in the trees. Their larvae has one of the longest development periods in the insect world – sixteen years. The combined racket of whirs and buzzes these harmless little bugs make is thought to be both a defence against birds and other predators and the mating call of the males. Note: In some parts of Africa they are known as Christmas Beetles.

Dense *miombo* in which elephant move like great shadows.

A wizened *mpingo* tree at the roadside. From its 'ebony' wood the Makonde carve their classically convoluted, two-tone images of folklore characters.

A V-shaped formation of sacred ibis over the river.

Out of canopies of dark clouds and a duck-egg green sky this evening, forked tongues of lightning and thunder on a Wagnerian scale.

Among the many weird aspects of the Selous to intrigue the visitor are the petrified forests, so ancient and authentic-looking that one expects to see prehistoric monsters living in them. Conifers and other trees have been laid bare by, according to scientists, 300 million years of tropical rainstorms.

I use a block of this petrified wood, amber in colour and as hard and heavy as marble, for a paperweight.

Magical? At night the only lights to be seen are those of winking fireflies and the coldly brilliant stars set in a dome of black velvet.

And fantastic. In the far south, precipitous red cliffs, formed by a geological fault, flank the valleys of the Luwegu river and its rhythmic-sounding tributaries, the Njenje, Mbarangandu and Lukala. Clinging to the cliffs are inaccessible patches of forest thought to contain wild flowers and shrubs unknown to botanists. The forests of

Sheltered by undergrowth, a hungry lioness gorges on a freshly killed impala.

the tall borassus palm and the alluvial flats around the rivers maintain hundreds of lion, elephant, rhino and buffalo, as well as sable antelope in numbers rarely seen elsewhere.

In some dry seasons, one can drive for a hundred miles along the sandy bed of the Mbarangandu. Like its sister-rivers, however, it becomes a sudden, roaring torrent after a deluge in the monsoon months.

A flash flood carrying tons of sand obliterated within two days all traces of a light aircraft that crash-landed on a bank of the Mbarangandu. Ground and air searchers could not find even a wheel.

Water is the key to the viability of the Selous. Its very being stems from the myriad lakes, rivers, streams and cold fresh springs that ensure adequate pasturage for the animals. Criss-crossing the reserve in a helicopter one afternoon I saw this pattern clearly, together with many of the 2,000 miles of sand and black-cotton soil trails – some of them overgrown and 'inoperable' – that, together with several airstrips, have been hacked out of the tangled bush during the last twenty-five years or so by the wardens and their men.

So dense is much of the bush that animals can disappear silently and within seconds. A glimpse of tusks at lower right indicates the closeness of a large elephant.

Bobbing and weaving low over the *miombo*, we played God as the helicopter set herds of elephant stampeding into the trees. Only a bull rhino, with a hide of armour-plating six million years old, stood his ground – his horn raised defiantly as he gazed myopically at the clattering bird-monster approaching. We zoomed overhead. He charged the air.

As the pilot followed the upstream course of the Rufiji a hundred feet from the ground, scores of crocodiles slithered into the water, and hippo in the shallows plunged to the safety of the deep in showers of glistening spray.

Emerging from a black rain-cloud, our helicopter circled the Shuguli Falls, a point of spectacular beauty in the broadest section – the pelican's pouch – of the Selous. The impact was stunning.

Just below us was the wild, seething confluence of the Kilombero and Luwega rivers amid the primitively sylvan setting of a *miombo* dotted with the pimples of volcanic cones.

The falls complex consists of a mile-long series of cataracts, miniature Niagaras framed by misty rainbows. Almost hidden in the foam-flecked waters of this giant's cauldron were flooded trees and rocky islets. Small wonder that 'Shuguli' is African for 'busy-ness'.

We veered away at last, and back-tracked to follow the Rufiji to a point in the north of the Selous where it makes a right-angle bend towards the sea. The river narrows there, racing over grim rocks in whirlpools and flurries of sepia suds through a steep wooded gorge named after a German geologist-explorer, Stiegler, and now the site of a lodge for 'adventure safaris'.

A £200 million dam may be built at this site to supply the Tanzanian capital with cheap hydro-electric power, creating a long narrow lake that would be an added tourist attraction with a new diversity of wild animals around its shores. It is not expected to produce insoluble environmental problems, provided the setting up of a mass of fishing villages by Africans is avoided by careful planning and subsequent management.

We landed on the heli-pad at Stiegler's Gorge, and a Norwegian consultant engineer drove me back cross-country to Karl's camp.

Karl had arranged a water expedition to get close-ups of some of the Selous' 50,000 'river horses', as the ancient Greeks called hippo, and the next day I clambered aboard his fourteen-foot dory. It had a 10 h.p. outboard, and a hunting rifle in the bows in case of emergency.

At that time speed-fiends could hire a 45 m.p.h. two-seater jet boat at the other Rufiji camp for their river-viewing, but we were able to drift in quietly among the hippo in our flat-bottom craft. We counted as many as forty or fifty in a group.

Harrumphing and snorting in the stream like Blimpish colonels or giving cavernous yawns, the 'river horses' look deceptively clownish and benign.

Now and then an old male guardian of a family – his flanks bearing the furrowed scars of titanic battles – would give a scary bellow of protest and charge towards us like an amphibian tank. Karl, barefoot in grey shorts and shirt, was quick on the throttle – putting the dory 'full ahead' for the middle of the river. These seemingly ungainly brutes, he said, were graceful swimmers in their underwater ballets. On land, where they feed at night on short juicy grasses, they can charge at a terrifying 30 m.p.h. if angry or frightened.

Further upstream, where palm trunks leaned drunkenly in the swiftly-flowing Rufiji like the masts of sunken ships, we spotted a group of crocs, some at least fifteen feet long. Sunning themselves on a silvery shore with jaws wickedly agape, they remained as immobile as if they had been modelled in bronze. Each had a small white bird, an egret, picking its rapier-sharp teeth for scraps of fish. Over 270 crocodiles have been counted recently on a stretch of the Rufiji less than a mile long.

On either bank, deep in the tawny grass, were large herds of the Selous' 150,000 buffalo, staring more with mild curiosity than hostility at us human intruders.

Wounded and dying, the 'buff' becomes a dangerous adversary, turning hunter and stalking the man who shot him. 'Seems the animal is determined to take mortal revenge,' said Karl.

Only three months before, an African professional hunter in the Selous had been killed in such a way. With infinite cunning and stealth, the animal he had shot in the shoulder made its way back around the hunter, charged him from behind and gored him as he lay on the ground.

Seen from a boat, the air or a safari truck, the Selous presents an infinite variety of fascinating and dramatic scenes. But, say the old hands, the best way to appreciate it is by just footslogging.

So, compass and maps in pocket, accompanied by an armed African guard named Hamisi, I set out one day, and quickly came to appreciate that in nature's kaleidoscope there is fragile beauty as well as blood and death.

Butterflies, their wing-tips violet or vivid tangerine, flitted among the ghostly trumpets of rain lilies in glades where shafts of sunlight made sparkling jewels of humming-birds and lilac-breasted rollers. Scarlet beetles scurried to the safety of rotting logs, and armoured millipedes went 'marching as to war' on all those legs.

Here was a tiny universe existing alongside our own. Beetles, birds and dragonflies became numberless adornments as we trudged over virgin terrain where no tribesman with bow and arrows nor domestic animal had ever wandered.

On open ground, two giraffe bulls fought in a grassy bowl over a winsome female who loped to and fro in slow motion and fluttered her sweeping chorus girl's eye lashes. The males thumped, pranced and kicked for half an hour until one sank to the ground exhausted. The victor nuzzled his prize, and they made off together. Giraffe, their coats shining and markings bold, are only found in the north.

Lunch of ham sandwiches under a wild chestnut was interrupted

In an algae-green pond hippo share their habitat with water birds which swim close by in search of food.

A crocodile – one of the flourishing population of the Rufiji – makes a dash for the water.

when I glanced up through the leaves. A young leopard was crouched in a fork of the tree, its sea-green eyes fixed on a lame zebra close by that had been deserted by its companions. Lunch came to an abrupt end as we moved to a safer spot.

Hamisi claimed later that a zebra's stripes were intended to produce optical illusions to confuse predators. The stripes of the Selous breed are narrower than those of zebra in other parts of the world.

That afternoon, we saw a hundred or more elephant grazing majestically in a swamp, their immense black bodies and slender tusks contrasting sharply with the vivid colour of the grass on which they were feeding.

Stiegler's Gorge on the Rufiji river – 'Stigo' to African game staff – may one day be the site of one of Africa's greatest dams.

I got close to a pair but when they caught my scent on the breeze they waded off, knee-deep, into the water. In times of flood, the Selous tuskers sometimes swim across the debris-strewn rivers with their trunks raised like periscopes above the tumbling waters.

We made camp – sleeping-bags on the ground and mosquito nets hung from the lower branches of a *mopani* – as the evening star came out, and grilled over a log fire the tasty elephant-snout fish that wiry little Hamisi had caught in a tarn we could see beyond the flickering flames.

As the shadows danced, he told stories of mythical beings whom Africans believe dwell in the Selous – pythons fifty feet long that turn into witches when the hyena howls twice, huge, rainbow-tinted tree frogs with diamonds for eyes, and a lake-dweller with three heads and the body of a shark.

I awoke later when the night was filled with what seemed to be the squeaking of a million mice. In the beam of the torch, I saw a female elephant feeding on the *mopani* leaves – her ears flapping and squeaking as she munched contentedly. At sun-up the next day I discovered the pug-marks of a lion around my mosquito netting. I was experiencing most of the eyeball-to-eyeball thrills of big-game hunting – without firing a shot!

We broke camp and moved on ... In the desolate Zongowari section of the reserve, we stumbled on what must be one of the loneliest graves in the world.

Here, with the wind for a dirge, lies that fearless hero of Victorian adventure stories, F. C. Selous. Today the cairn of stones has disappeared and he is buried beneath a cracked and weathered slab of concrete that has a plaque with a simple, embossed cross. Now and then a bunch of wild daisies withers on the grave. No one knows who puts them there. Near the grave are the shallow trenches, overgrown with weeds, of von Lettow's *askaris*, one of whom had laid Selous low.

Gazing round this desolate corner of a foreign field, I noticed a small object in the rough grass. It was a mildewed .303 cartridge case, a relic of a Kaiser's dream of a Teutonic empire and, like the shell-cases, rusty horseshoes and hand grenades elsewhere in the Selous, of a hard-fought, honourable campaign.

From this sombre spot we travelled down to Kingupira, a collection of tin-roofed, single-storey buildings, site of the Miombo Research Institute (with its 150 yellowed elephant skulls ranged outside on the grass like an odd garden sculpture) and gateway to the southern Selous. From here our tortuous route took us through eerie tangled woods with only an occasional glade to relieve the claustrophobia.

Encamped far south by a river, the saucer-size spoor of big lions were everywhere. Hippo, leaving pad-and-toenail patterns on the bank (where sweet cool water was obtained merely by scraping a hole in the sand), snorted and grunted around us all night. At one time a huge crocodile and its attendant offspring slithered by in the moon-light, a few yards from the tent.

The ebony, or mpingo, *is beloved by the woodcarvers of the Makonde tribe.*

OVERLEAF: *An elephant looking prehistoric, crossing a river.*

Back at Karl's bar some days later, I met Alan Rodgers, a lecturer in the University of Dar es Salaam's department of zoology, who was for ten years (until 1976) a game research officer in the Selous based at Kingupira. Pleasantly brisk, he is one of the foremost authorities on the reserve and unique in the number of years he had devoted to it in the cause of science.

Old, infertile soils, he said, made the Selous useless for agriculture. The tsetse prevented cattle-raising and, to complete the reserve's isolation, the massive Rufiji river basin with its great tributaries made effective communications very difficult in times of flood.

'With its size and diversity of habitats and species, the Selous acts as a huge ecological reservoir and genetic store-house. It is a land and resource bank for the future when villagers can crop animals for food in adjacent buffer areas.'

Rodgers believes Tanzania's socialist policy of uprooting remote African families and putting them in extensive co-operative (*ujamaa*) settlements with schools and dispensaries, helps to preserve the Selous – one of the least scientifically researched territories in Africa.

He has counted in the reserve 350 different bird species, and among the 2,000 plant species there he has found at least 40 new to science.

Selous zebra is a species related to, and belonging to, the Burchell's zebra but the Selous zebra have narrower stripes.

The rains that have changed the Rufiji's water course have also profoundly affected the landscape. In time the borassus palms lose their heads and die.

Up to now few scientists have been prepared to face the challenges and rigours of the Selous with its wilderness, its demands on the human spirit and its remoteness. Geographically, the Selous flora has links with the north and south. Riverine and clay-soil thickets have many similarities with the Kenya coast, and the flora with that of Mozambique. The woodlands have many species in common with Zambia.

'On the other hand, when I was doing an ecological study of what the Selous wild animals eat, my researches were incomplete in many cases because I found that most of the grasses on which the grazers fed had no names. To confuse matters further, I've collected flower and plant species there that were previously known only in Somalia, northern Kenya, Zaire and Angola.'

Geographical oddities concern the animals too. Rodgers said roan antelope, so typical of *miombo* woodland, was completely absent, as were ostrich and the tiny dik-dik antelope. Giraffe were restricted to the north, not daring to cross the Rufiji which also acted as a barrier for certain types of wildebeest.

'Cheetah are rarely seen, and are probably only permanently resident on the more open plains of the north-east. Side-striped jackal

101

are associated with hum. settlement all around the Selous but have only been sighted three or four times in the reserve itself – a particularly peculiar distribution pattern.'

Rodgers and ex-warden Brian Nicholson feel only those areas like the Selous that are free from competition and are big enough for the game populations to remain unaffected by what goes on outside their borders will survive. They see the Selous as 'Africa untouched by the twentieth century' where many mysteries of bird and insect life, and of the flora, await revelation to the world by intrepid explorers.

The auburn-haired hospital nurse from Nottingham, pouring a 'Kilimanjaro' lager at Karl's camp at the end of a week's stay, admitted she had no head for ecosystem statistics, water tables and soil counts. She just *knew* the Selous would be the last wild animal sanctuary on earth.

The rains have started – it is November – and the Shuguli waterfalls to the south and west of the reserve, where the Kilombero river meets the Luwegu river are a frantic pattern of lacy water and ancient rock.

10. The New Hunters

ANIMALS IN ABUNDANCE have long attracted both trophy-hunters with big bank balances and humble poachers to the Selous.

It has forty-six hunting blocks, each measuring an average of 300 square miles, that were first mapped out by Brian Nicholson and Allen Rees working on a principle of scientific wildlife management that had no place for sentimentality. They disregarded – Rees, reluctantly, until he saw the positive benefits – the bankrupt theory that hunting in a game reserve was a contradiction in terms and together they developed the Selous' extraordinary wildlife population on the basis that hunting for pleasure and conservation do not conflict.

'The limited hunting quotas laid down for each block represent a very small proportion of the game, predators and prey in each,' says Nicholson. 'They are, in fact, animals which are expendable.'

Selous himself never hunted over the ground that became 'his' reserve. He is reputed to have called the region 'the most pestilential place on earth'. That, however, was when he had to endure the miseries and hardships of war there.

Others who came much later had 'marvellous sport', like Terry Irwin who left the Game Department, a year after his colleagues had drawn up their 'management complex' in 1962, to become a white hunter in the Selous. He took with him in his new career the name *Kiboroso*, 'The One Who Drags Us', that had been given him by his black game scouts.

'Well, it was more of a compliment than a criticism,' he chuckles. 'I had saved these chaps' lives quite a few times on patrol by dragging them to water when they were at the point of collapse. They would not have survived in the bush if I hadn't pulled them along.'

Terry remembers his hunting days in the Selous as 'great', 'memorable' and 'exciting'.

'Camp supplies came in by lorry; the clients and spare parts arrived by air. These people, aristocrats, filmstars, tycoons and so on, had only about one thing in common. They were rich beyond *my* wildest dreams. 'My most appreciative clients, perhaps, were a Texan oil millionaire and his pretty wife. They loved every minute of their safari

A nursery of young giraffe. The habitat of all Selous giraffe is solely north of the Rufiji river.

and promised to come back the following year. They never turned up. I learned subsequently that she had murdered him and then committed suicide.'

He says casually that 'quite a few' of the trophies his clients obtained in the Selous were world records at the time.

All animals not on the game quota list such as cheetah (rare even in the Selous) and giraffe, were 'not to be molested in any way' according to the regulations. There was an annual quota of rhino that could be shot, specifically allocated to certain blocks where these animals were relatively numerous.

On the quota list then, as now, were elephant, buffalo, lion, leopard, eland, greater kudu, sable, zebra, common wildebeest, waterbuck, hippo, reedbuck, impala, bushbuck, bushpig, hyena, rock rabbit (hyrax), baboon and serval cat. No one was allowed to shoot more than one of any species.

Most of the animals were obtainable in every block, except for sable, waterbuck and impala which were protected in certain blocks but could be hunted in others.

A handsome male waterbuck, one of a healthy population in the Selous.

The 'Big Five' have remained plentiful throughout the Selous and, except for the reserve's 5,000 rhino (now a nationally protected animal), can be hunted widely.

'Elephant with good tusks were everywhere,' Terry added. 'Although those in the Selous are smaller in body size than others in Tanzania, their tusks tend to grow comparatively longer – a few up to ten feet. Tusks of more than a hundred pounds each have been obtained on some safaris. An American housewife shot one specimen whose single tusk – the other had broken off at the root – weighed ninety-one pounds.'

Terry Irwin and his clients encountered buffalo in herds of up to a thousand. A record 'buff' trophy on one of his expeditions was 50¾ inches. Its horns encompassed three men standing together in front of the dead animal.

'Lions are generally easy to obtain. Some fine-maned specimens that also went into the record books were shot in the Selous in my time. Leopard occur in all blocks. The Somali type with fine, small rosettes on their skin are comparatively common.'

An adolescent male lion, whose mane has still to develop.

Eland trophies of thirty inches and longer, sable of forty inches, were often bagged. Game birds provided a welcome change on the camp menus and there were flocks of quail, guinea fowl, francolin (something of an African pheasant), ducks and geese for the guns to bring down over both land and water.

The classic hunting pose: (l. to r.) client, gun bearer and professional hunter, with their trophy: a fine buffalo.
Terry Irwin.

The careers of Terry and others as professional hunters in Tanzania came to an abrupt end in September 1973. Every type of hunting, whether for sport or food, was banned to allow the undisturbed breeding of wild animals throughout the country (although those in the Selous were not in danger) and to enable the government to step up its never-ending war against poaching.

The ban was to stay in operation for five years. When it was lifted, hunting was restricted to six months annually instead of being allowed all the year round. And the dashing white hunters of books and screen, whom F. C. Selous and others who followed him represented, were replaced by Africans – fully-fledged professionals in their own country. Their fathers or uncles may have been one of the sweating, semi-naked porters who carried crates of ammunition, camp equipment and stacks of high-velocity rifles on their heads through the waist-high elephant grass on safari in the bad old colonial days. But those days are not *quite* over – an American writer walking in the Selous a few months ago had seven Africans carrying his gear.

This new breed, the black 'white hunter', was being trained before and during the suspension of hunting, at first in the Tanzanian northern town of Arusha, exactly halfway between the Cape of Good Hope and Cairo, and later at Mweka Wildlife Management College near Moshi at the foot of Kilimanjaro. They were to join a national organization which alone can take out sport hunters for fees.

With safari overheads, licences and other hunting charges, it can cost around £8,000 to shoot a trophy elephant or one of the Selous' lions. An elderly Italian from Verona paid £250 a day not long ago to shoot big game in the southern Selous from a hunting car; he had a wooden leg. Yet Tanzania has more applications from abroad for hunting trips than she is willing, or able, to accommodate.

In the early seventies Tanzania produced Africa's first black professional hunter in 34-year-old Saidi Kawawa, younger brother of the country's then Second Vice-President and son of a game ranger. True to type, he was handsome, and had all the qualifications of his white colleagues.

Kawawa, who has since become leader of a corps of Tanzanian hunters, was given his coveted and hard-won hunter's licence after passing a stiff examination at the Arusha training school that was another first-of-its-kind in the world. He and his fellow trainees, including a former gun-bearer and an ex-policeman, led the erosion of the exclusive fraternity of white hunters – one of the last colour preserves in independent Africa.

With the hunter's eleventh commandment of 'Thou Shalt Not Miss' drummed into them, they had played practical, turnabout games of hunter and client in the Selous, tracked wounded animals, battled with fellow pupils impersonating poachers, lived off the land, shot sick hippo from a canoe hollowed out of a tree trunk, read the stars, given First Aid to the injured, and stalked big game by spoor and trail signs.

In the lecture rooms of Arusha, they learned map reading, fauna conservation, the rudiments of taxidermy, game geography, and how to operate radio-phones or bait clearings for lion and leopard. On the rifle range, they were obliged to hit the bulls-eye with every shot. They had to acquire a 'conversational' knowledge of world affairs, music, literature, religion and sport. It was important too, apparently, to know how to mix a *very* dry Martini at the end of every day's hunt. Each pupil worked to an inflexible criterion: 'If I were a client, would I hire me as a professional hunter?'

Among the aspirants on a later course, at the Mweka college, was dapper Daniel Tarimo, who currently organizes government-operated 'foto-safaris' in the Selous and other game preserves.

OVERLEAF: *Eland are plentiful in the Selous and, in September, have numerous young.*

Part of young Daniel's training was a week sleeping rough in the Selous on an elephant control operation. His instructor was a chubby

109

amiable sharpshooter – Ernest Hemingway's son, Pat. He had taken a job at the college after a spell as an unsuccessful white hunter among the 'green hills of Africa' in northern Tanzania. Working in his father's 'un-hunted pocket in the million miles of bloody Africa', Pat found he loathed most of his safari clients who, he once told me, tended to treat him 'like a goddam butler'.

Daniel Tarimo, easy-going and personable, did not have the same fervent prejudice against the rich and on the whole enjoyed his work with them. An instinctively able tracker like his fellow Africans, he takes pride in the fact that professional hunters play an important role in keeping down human predators, scaring them away from the game blocks or reporting to the authorities by runner or radio-telephone such signs of their presence as beehive-shaped shelters made of branches or the still-warm ashes of cooking fires.

Poaching was at its worst in the Selous in the days of the British about twenty years ago when, owing to a skeleton staff, ranger and game scout patrols were few and far between.

Elephant, rhino and crocodile were the chief targets of native poachers, who trekked long distances into the Selous on foot or were lucky enough to own lorries and quick-firing modern weapons for their gruesome trade. Casual poaching for the pot – and relatives back home – by wandering Wangindo had little adverse effect on the game populations, but full-time poachers were a menace.

Elephant were shot down with guns or poisoned arrows, for their tusks which, at night, were loaded aboard dhows hidden in the mangrove swamps of the Rufiji delta. Rhino were trapped in deep pits or steelwire nooses. Their horns, ground to a powder, fetched thousands of pounds in the Far East. Although there is absolutely no foundation for the belief, elderly merchants were convinced (and still are) that sprinkled over, say, sharkfin soup the powder is a powerful aphrodisiac. As a result of this, the price of rhino horn has quadrupled in the course of time and has brought most of Africa's rhino outside the Selous to the point of extinction.

Impala in forest.

Crocodile were attacked too, and their killers baited steel hooks with haunches of gazelle and attached them by hawsers to oil-drum buoys in the rivers and lakes. The reptiles are slaughtered for their soft and durable belly-skins which are used to make expensive shoes, women's handbags and wallets.

Between operations, the poachers harpooned the big catfish with their long-bladed spears. Strips of the flesh, salted and sun-dried like the *biltong* meat of the old Boer fighters, were carried as hard rations.

The sections of the Selous most badly affected by poaching in those earlier days were in the north and west, and it was not remedied until the administration of the reserve was centralized after *uhuru*.

The rangers had been handicapped in their operations against poachers by lack of water transport. When Allen Rees acquired a rubber dinghy, the peaceful existence of those who had established themselves on river islands in the guise of fishermen came to an end.

Later, he got larger craft equipped with outboard motors and used them up-river to seize bands of poachers who were killing hippo for their teeth which, because they look like ivory, finally ended up as tourists' gee-gaws in the curio trade.

'At one time,' he recalls, 'I surprised a campful of these chaps and some runaway elephant poachers who had abandoned their ivory, food and cooking utensils at a tributary to the Muhangasi river. I tracked them down with my handbearing compass, and this eventually gained quite a reputation among Africans as an anti-poaching weapon.'

From mid-1962 to the end of 1963 there were nearly 2,000 convictions for poaching in the Selous. Tons of wire snares were recovered, miles of snare-fences destroyed and over 200 assorted firearms confiscated, along with a vast quantity of more primitive weapons. The big gangs were broken up – often caught intact – but not without dire casualties to the game staff.

According to a post-independence official report: 'The poaching fraternity became thoroughly demoralized.'

A minority kept up their activities on a wide scale until the early seventies, when a tough young American looking for adventure named Jon Speed offered his services as an anti-poaching officer under Brian Nicholson, the then head of all game wardens. Speed, an Arizonian, was signed on and trained a staff of resourceful and efficient game scouts. His party trick after a year or two was to creep up to an elephant and pull its tail. The foolhardy act could mean a ghastly death by being trampled underfoot but Speed knew his bushcraft and that an elephant rarely sees or hears an approach, relying on its sense of smell as a downwind warning.

'The black men who work in the field get very little credit,' he says. 'but they are the men who save the game and not the people who sit in offices framing policies.'

Having got his team together, Jon Speed arrested gangs of poachers who came from villages around the reserve – until he found out that the local magistrate was a member of one of the poaching rings.

Speed's technique was to attack a poachers' camp with two or three of his men in the middle of the night. 'Gunfire and yelling was enough to send the bad men running. We would set the camp ablaze and confiscate the poachers' canoes for our own use. I'd yell into the swamps and tell them to surrender or we would leave them to their fate. Some gave themselves up, but others never got out of the morass alive.'

He would fly over the Selous with Nicholson to look for poachers. 'They'd wave to me, not knowing that in a few hours I'd be there by boat or Land-Rover to attack them.'

During his two years in the Selous, Speed was attacked many times by hippo and his boats destroyed. 'One time on patrol I ran into a school of sleeping hippo and lost everything. Boat, tent, rifle, compass and food. It took me three days to walk and swim out of that swamp. I

A swallowtail butterfly: the Papilio antheus.

had only brackish water to keep me going and I was eaten alive by mosquitoes.'

With poachers relatively few in number these days, the Selous game scouts – some of them reformed illegal hunters who know all the tricks of the business – have been given only bicycles, dug-out canoes and World War I rifles to keep the criminals at bay. A typical Tanzanian game scout, in a threadbare shirt, sandals and shorts, has to keep two wives and seven children on £20 a month. The country can afford no more.

Emmanuel Kadiva, twenty-five, is keen to give them a hand in a year or so, when he finishes his Mweka course to become the youngest professional hunter in Tanzania.

Of fine physique, neatly dressed in a wind-cheater and blue jeans, a lion's tooth on a gold chain round his neck, Emmanuel is a good example of the black 'white hunter' of tomorrow. He spent his boyhood on the slopes of Mount Kilimanjaro and has been fascinated by hunting since he was a secondary school pupil in Tanzania.

'My heroes were the Europeans – romantic figures to boys all over the world – who ran those safaris. I saw every film about them and big game hunting that I could. Friends of the family, who were already hunters, told me about the life, and I became more and more enthusiastic. During school holidays, I went out duck shooting or spent hours in national parks just looking at the animals and learning their ways.'

In Mweka's classrooms Emmanuel studies ballistics, wild animal diseases, botany, natural history and range ecology as well as the broad techniques of hunting. His charm of manner comes naturally.

Emmanuel thinks the best type of professional hunter should have the same qualifications as an experienced game warden. 'Although depending on wild animals for food doesn't apply to most of my people any more, bushcraft, of course, is in my blood. I can spot animals quickly over long distances, and I know just where to find them.'

He smiles and adds with patent sincerity: 'Hunting can be risky so you have to have a real feeling for it as a career. It's not just a routine job with a good salary.'

Fluent in English and Swahili, he has been looking for pen-friends overseas to increase his day-to-day knowledge of international affairs in anticipation of the day when he will have to discuss the world with his foreign clients.

Before he takes out his first booking, Emmanuel will have to work for six months as an assistant to senior men who have been hunting with Americans, British and Germans in the Selous since the general ban on the sport ended.

A textile manufacturer from Hamburg, who engaged the services of one of these men for a month, said: 'He was first-rate, a fine shot and a good companion. I learned more about African animals from him than I would in a pile of books. We had terrific sport. I found the Selous is the only place in Africa where you can bag a whole range of big game in a few weeks.'

It is more than that. The reserve is one of the few African areas open to the hunter that possesses a game population many times greater than it had when the first Europeans penetrated the continent.

'There is no place left where lion and leopard occur in such numbers,' Brian Nicholson maintains. 'Only a few of the parts now divided into quota blocks would have been worth visiting for trophy hunting twenty or so years ago. Today most of the blocks can each take two or three hunting safaris a year.'

11. 'Lions Build Schools'

He is a full-blooded Maasai warrior and the holder of a Bachelor of Arts degree. He can 'talk' to lions, a trick of grunts and clicks which he learned the hard way – as a barefoot boy in a few wisps of flame-coloured calico herding cattle out on the plain.

After independence, he became the first black Conservator – a benign overlord – of Tanzania's olympian Ngorongoro Crater, a ninth wonder of the world, where his statuesque people, smeared from head to foot in red ochre and river mud, live alongside a host of wild beasts.

Once, but no more, Maasai youths like him were obliged to kill a lion single-handed to prove their manhood.

Solomon Alexander Ole Saibull, forty-five, is today Tanzania's Minister for Natural Resources and Animal Production.

When I first met him in the famous crater ten years ago, *Ndugu* (Citizen, Comrade or Mister) Saibull's 'uniform' was a pair of baggy trousers, an olive-green shirt, brogues and an old yellow pullover. As singularly sincere and unaffected as ever, he now has modestly-furnished offices in Dar as his headquarters. He wears neither some faintly Ruritanian outfit nor a Maasai orange shirt, but in deference to his elevation to Cabinet rank he has abandoned the threadbare sweater for a pearl-grey safari suit. His sense of humour and air of good fellowship remain the same.

A nature-lover since childhood, the minister responsible for Tanzania's wild animals cares deeply about them and their natural environment. He is infinitely happier out in the bush than sitting at a desk in the city with a pile of statistical reports and conference minutes in front of him.

So it is natural that the Selous is his special concern. He is well to the fore of those convinced it will continue to flourish while many other game reserves and national parks on the African continent are in danger of extinction at the hands of man.

We talked of this over mugs of coffee when the minister visited the Selous towards the end of my stay. 'Corruption, large-scale poaching and human pressures are the three greatest threats to all the other animal sanctuaries,' he said. 'As you'll have seen, there's no wholesale poaching here such as you find in most parts of Africa with any

Kongoni or hartebeest framed by young trees.

animals left. In consequence, there's very little corruption.

'There are no major animal migrations out of the Selous on the scale of that yearly exodus from our Serengeti national park of wildebeest and zebra in search of water. That always attracts hundreds of poachers.

'Again, there is no erosion here by land-hungry peoples.'

The minister picked up his binoculars and surveyed a brood of wild goslings waddling ashore from the river through a clump of reeds. 'You know, a lot of the colonial administrators thought one of the first things African states would do after *uhuru* would be to destroy their wildlife – gobble it up. The speculation was that we would have no room for the conservation of animals nor understand the economic value of them to tourism.

He swept his arm around, and went on: 'Well, the Selous represents more than six per cent of our land surface and a quarter of the country is devoted to national parks, game reserves and "No shooting" areas. Those figures speak for themselves, don't they? From the president down, we have a commitment to preserve wildlife at all costs and on a priority basis, even at the expense of some other goals.'

Tanzania, he said, spends on an average four per cent of its national budget on conservation.

'I think that figure is one of the highest in the world. Why, only five years ago, the United States, the world's richest nation, spent a mere .08 per cent for the same purpose.'

Looking back to the twenties, *Ndugu* Saibull said he believed the main preoccupations of desk-bound colonial officials responsible for natural resources, were the control of dangerous wild animals and the hunting of a wide range of others 'as targets in a shooting game or pastime'.

He added: 'Well, the days of the exclusively "white hunter" are over. At least, we don't have them in Tanzania. We have only professional hunters who can be white or black – but they must be Tanzanian citizens. That's only fair. There's no question of a colour bar or that sort of thing.

'And we are now trying in our wildlife management research and teaching programmes to place much greater emphasis on conservation and far less on sport hunting or the direct utilization of animals for their skins. It is a philosophy of conservation. We have replaced the word "game" with "wildlife" in all our official dealings, as a gesture of respect for the living resources we are conserving.'

Why then was hunting in the Selous so actively encouraged?

'Basically,' he replied, 'for the purpose of animal population control in the interest of the reserve, and then for revenue it brings.'

Strictly managed hunting, he said, was part of conservation where the habitat might be threatened by excessive numbers of a particular species using it. Animals had to be kept in balance with the environment. At the same time, profits from the expensive recreation of big game hunting were ploughed back into conservation.

Warthog are common in the Selous and are especially numerous near Kingupira. To eat, they go on their knees.

'It's our policy to protect and manage the wildlife resource in order to generate other long-term benefits. Where a tourist's pound or dollar is concerned, lions build schools and hippos hospitals.

'On the other hand, human and monetary costs in conservation have been considerable. Quite a few people have lost their lives in the cause of conservation in Tanzania. Some of them were gored by charging buffalos; others were bitten by leopards or venomous snakes, drowned in flooded rivers, or died in motor or aircraft accidents. And there were those who died from the poisoned arrows or bullets of merciless poachers.

'I feel, quite deeply, that the least we who have survived can do for all these and others who have lost their lives in the cause of conservation, is to make sure that what they died for lives on.'

To that end, Tanzania has taken stock of its laws, regulations and institutions relating to wildlife and has strengthened them over the past few years.

119

Conservation is being fostered in a broad sense, educating the public on the subject through films, slides, radio and TV programmes and the Press. Young people are being urged to form wildlife conservation clubs in schools, colleges and university.

A national wildlife protection force has been formed, a wildcat band of 210 militarily-trained rangers equipped with sophisticated weapons and communications 'to match and beat today's kind of poacher in our country'. Where the value of 'illegal trophies' (be they rhino horns, a cheetah skin or elephant tusks), exceeds £1,000, the *minimum* prison sentence is now three years and a fine of up to £5,000. Poachers are listed in a rogues' gallery, with mug shots and personal records, for ease of detection in future cases.

As the minister recalled, before all this, in the days of the colonialists, native poachers treated customary prison sentences of a few weeks with light-hearted contempt, even appreciation. Given a break from their hazardous occupation, a roof over their heads and two meals a day, prison to them was 'King George hoteli'. Long and ⅃rous jail terms are now proving a deterrent.

'There are so many conflicting schools of thought on the question of wildlife,' says Solomon Saibull. 'There are the animal killers and harvesters who see in every moving animal either a trophy target or pounds of meat, ivory or trophies. There are the lovers and protectors of wild animals who accord the same sanctity to them as they do to people. There are the conservators who see in conservation a unique opportunity for some scientific contribution, cultural revival and wise utilization on a sustained yield basis.

'In our country, wildlife conservation and utilization is part and parcel of a long-term national development strategy. Naturally, we want to achieve self-sufficiency in food, shelter and clothing – the principal priorities – but at the same time we want to keep an adequately rich natural environment for ourselves and all who come after us.

'In a primitive society, man's effort to obtain food is minimal. It involves the gathering of fruits, the picking of leaves and the digging up of roots for the agriculturist. It means the making of stone choppers, hand axes and stone slings for the "industrialist". It means the hunting of rabbits, gazelle or deer, and progressively bigger and more dangerous animals for the "rancher".

'Between primitive man and today's modern agriculturist, industrialist and rancher, there are various stages through which the cultivator, the tool maker, and the cattle-herder passes in trying to do more in order to satisfy his needs. But, for the most part, man's path is without the advantage of wide enough knowledge, or deep enough sensitivity, to enable him to be sure that more effort at development must be matched with greater caution for better overall results.

'He breaks the soil without caring about erosion, indeed often he facilitates it. He obtains construction materials without giving a thought to the replacement process of those materials, let alone

The extraordinary grace and beauty of an impala in action.

worrying about re-cycling the same materials for use again and again. He expands acreages single-mindedly without regard for the trees he cuts down, the forests he destroys, the barrenness of the land he causes, or the possibility of creating a desert – literally and metaphorically – and bringing about total destruction in the name of development.'

Criticizing his own pastoral Maasai, the minister said that for the herdsman, the story was similar. He kept his cattle in ever-growing numbers which were little used, and confined them in too small an area, too long, without a thought about the tremendous damage he was causing to the pasture, the soil and the silting downstream. He lit fires without worrying about the fate of the microscopic soil organisms, or useful bacteria, which were so vital for the life of any grazing population, including his cattle. He moved with his herds through mile upon mile, while setting new claims upon natural and as yet good land, and he destroyed pasture and soil in his trail, again in the name of development.

'The same applies to the tool maker; the manufacturer; the industrialist; the road maker; the layer of power pylons, telephone lines, and sewage systems; the builder of skyscrapers; the ship builder, and the designer of supersonic aircraft – the lot. All this is definitely a form of "development".

But must development be intertwined with destruction?

'I don't think so. The choice is not between development with destruction and no development at all. Development should be

inimical to destruction. Development should be far-sighted and wholesome. Development can be achieved by proper planning, by giving maximum possible respect to natural phenomena, by intelligent use and protection of resources – in short, by blending development with conservation.

'It is in man's own interest that, in whatever he does, once he is no longer a slave to his primitivity, he should aim at development without destruction. Of course, it's almost a platitude to say this, but there is value in stating and re-stating the obvious, for I'm not at all sure that what is obvious to one is always obvious to many others. At any rate, I am quite certain that the values of conservation, and respect for the natural environment, which is vital for providing inspiration and guidance for sensible development, have not been all that widely appreciated in the world up to now.'

We strolled together to the minister's Land-Rover with its official crest on the doors.

'I'm often assured we're head and shoulders above anybody else in protecting wildlife. That's particularly gratifying to me.'

We shook hands and he climbed into the Land-Rover beside the

A bloom as bright as a buttercup. This flower is of the Tricliceras *species.*

122

Impala and their young, which are notable for their gawky charm.

driver, then turned to me through the open window. 'For all that, we've got to remember that the Selous and, in fact, all other outstanding wonders of nature wherever they may be, are not just the heritages of the countries in which they are located,' he said. 'They are of immeasurable value, surely, to all mankind, and therefore the countries that possess these living treasures are custodians of the world for all time.'

He waved and smiled as the vehicle drove off. A canopy of dust over the *bundu* swirled and grew fainter . . .

12. 'Kwaheri'

I LEFT THE Selous the same way I had arrived – on the railroad that passes through its northern tip.

It was evening by the time I reached Fuga, and all around were towering castles of cloud above a gaudy, picture-postcard sunset that turned the leaves of the acacias into filigree and threw the indigo peaks in the far distance into cardboard-cutout relief.

Somewhere in that back of beyond, I reflected, two leopard sisters with their four cubs (of whom I had heard but never seen) might be gazing with slit-eyes into the gloaming. On the lakes of burnished pewter, pelicans with their plumage painted silver by the dying sun would be dipping their beaks in unison as they fished in flotilla formations for fingerlings of bream.

A throaty blast from the siren of the train's diesel locomotive as it drew in sent a family of warthogs, cousins of the wild boars of eastern Europe, scampering into the scrubland with their whiplash tails erect in alarm.

I took my seat under a whirring fan in a compartment of polished chrome and battleship grey with a slatted wooden door. A bushy-maned male, two females and five cubs in a pride of lion lay sprawled in the brassy twilight under a candelabrum of euphorbia flanking the arrow-straight track.

Perhaps anticipating a meal from a kill, a scrawny-necked vulture soared overhead.

As the train glided out of the station to begin its nine-stop journey to Dar, the scarlet hibiscus on the platform – a 'Chinese Rose' full blown at noon – was slowly folding its petals for the night.

Impala grazing peacefully in open country on either side of the rails became swiftly-vanishing tan shapes as we gathered speed. A string of cantering zebra lost the race and wheeled away.

The train click-clacked over the invisible demarcation line of the Selous on its way to flat coastal countryside and the clustered lights of Dar reflected in a darkening faraway sky.

It was *kwaheri* (goodbye) to an enchanted wilderness where the unsullied tapestry of interdependence of all living things from the tiniest midge to the oldest elephant patriarch is indeed a 'rich and precious inheritance'.

Silhouettes: black poles and soft fronds of borassus palms.

125

The black and gold canopy of an African sunset.

Bibliography

Dorst & Dandelot: *The Larger Mammals of Africa*, Collins, 1970

Hatch, John : *Tanzania – A Profile*, Pall Mall Press, 1972

Hargreaves, Dorothy & Bob: *African Trees*, Hargreaves Co., U.S.A., *c.* 1970

Ionides, C.J.P.: *A Hunter's Story*, W.H. Allen, 1965

Lettow-Vorbeck, General Paul von: *My Reminiscences of East Africa*, Hurst & Blackett, 1920

Miller, Charles: *Battle for the Bundu*, Macdonald & Jane, 1974

Maberly, C.T. Astley: *Animals of East Africa*, Hodder & Stoughton, 1971

Millais, J.G.: *Life of Frederick Courteney Selous, D.S.O.*, Longmans, Green, 1919

Nicholson, Brian: *The Selous Game Reserve*, Monograph, 1970

Pretorius, Major P.J.: *Jungle Man*, Dutton, 1948

Reader, J & Croze, H. *Pyramids of Life*, Collins, 1977

Roosevelt, Theodore: *African Game Trails*, Scribner, 1910

Selous, F.C.: *Travel and Adventures in South-East Africa*, Rowland Ward, 1893

　African Nature Notes and Reminiscences, Macmillan, 1908

　A Hunter's Wanderings in Africa, Bentley, 1881

Williams, J.G.: *The Birds of East and Central Africa*, Collins, 1963